Twelve Months of Spiritual Fruit Maturing

BUT THE FRUIT OF THE SPIRIT IS

LOVE

JOY

PEACE

LONGSUFFERING

GENTLENESS

GOODNESS

FAITH

MEEKNESS

TEMPERANCE

AGAINST SUCH THERE IS NO LAW!

GALATIANS 5:22-23

Dr. Catherine Braswell

Printed in the United States of America

ISBN:	Softcover	978-1-63871-855-0
	Hardcover	978-1-63871-857-4
	eBook	978-1-63871-856-7

Republished by: PageTurner Press and Media LLC
Publication Date: 01/07/2022

To order copies of this book, contact:
PageTurner Press and Media
Phone: 1-888-447-9651
info@pageturner.us
www.pageturner.us

CONTENTS

To my husband Varick, my children, Andrea, James, and Kenneth. Thank you for being there for me all the times. I love you all very much.

INTRODUCTION

When talking to many Christians, I have noticed that they are having problems maturing in their spiritual walk. They speak of their love for the Lord, but cannot seem to be able to love one another or get alone with others as being a Christian. Many will say "it takes a lot to get along with people and they don't think that they can do it." The truth of the matter is, without Christ working through the Holy Spirit in us it will not happen. Some things we cannot obtain without the help of God. Walking in the Spirit is one of those things.

When you and I allow the Holy Spirit to mature the Fruit of the Spirit in us we will be able to do all the things Christ wants us to do. It is the power of God and not of ourselves that the fruit of the Spirit matures. Of course, it takes us agreeing and allowing the Holy Spirit to work in us. God has given us everything we need to make this a reality.

In this book I would like to use the Holy Scriptures through the Spirit of God, to help us work on maturing "The Fruit of the Spirit" in our lives. I would like for each of us to take one month at a time to diligently focus and work on each fruit as the Spirit begin the maturing process. Today let us get ready for a transformation in the way we walk in the Spirit and watch our fruit mature.

Month One - Why is it Important to Mature my Fruit?

Scripture text for reference and discussion

John 15:1-5

1)-I am the true vine, and my father is the husbandman. 2)-Every branch in me that beareth not fruit he taketh away: and every branch that beareth fruit, he purgeth it, that it may bring forth more fruit. 3)-Now you are clean through the word which I have spoken unto you. 4)-Abide in me, and I in you. As the branch cannot bear fruit of itself, except it abide in the vine; no more can ye, except ye abide in me. 5)-I am the vine, ye are the branches: He that abideth in me, and I in him, the same bringeth forth much fruit: for without me ye can do nothing.

As Christians, it is so very important that we understand the need of having a productive life in Christ. Even the holy Scriptures (Bible) teaches us in John 15:1-5 about Jesus being the true vine (source of power) and His Father, God is the husband (vine dresser or keeper). Showing the unified relationship between the Father and His Son staying connected with one another. Therefore, Jesus will complete everything His Father commands Him to do. This is the relationship you and I need in order to produce fruit in Christ.

Jesus calls Christians the branches. Telling us that if we do not stay connected to Him, (the vine) we can do nothing. What a powerful message this is to know that it is in my own interest that I stay connected to the (True Vine) Jesus.

Please understand that Jesus was getting ready to face death for the sins of the world and he knew that many were still rejecting Him. His disciples were getting ready to face a very hard place in their lives because of his crucifixion. Now Jesus needed to let them know about staying connected to Him and His Father so that they would have a productive and successful Ministry and life.

Jesus had come into the world to save everyone. These same people were rejecting Him and His message of salvation. Jesus knew His earthly time was drawing near and there was still so very much teaching that His disciples needed. So now He begin to teach them about the important need of bearing fruit for His kingdom.

When Jesus talks about bearing fruit for Him, He is referring to (bearing) making converts, walking in righteousness, and having Christian character, such as the fruit of the Spirit. Why is this so important? We must possess godly character to be able to offer the same to others.

Jesus explains to His disciples that every branch in Him that does not bear fruit, or shall I say that is not productive, He takes it away. We must realize that these branches are in Him. Meaning these are Christians that are not producing fruit. Sure, they are Christians but for some reasons they are not fruitful. I must ask myself, "am I fruitful?" I must look very honestly into my heart and see what I am doing in the area of fruit production. As Jesus disciples we are to always be productive. We must keep in close contact with Jesus so that our walk with Him will produce fruit. Jesus requires this of all Christians, not just their leaders.

Think about this, what if you had a fruit tree and you took great care of that tree from the time you planted it up until it was grownup. Each year during harvest time you noticed there were never any fruit on the tree. Would you not become concerned about that tree and wonder what else could you do differently to that tree to make it productive? Continuing to cultivate the tree doing everything possible to make it produce, how long would you continue spending time, money, and effort on that tree before you decide to get rid of it? How long? You would expect a return for the investments you placed into that tree.

We cannot continue to be unproductive in the work of the Lord and expect it to be okay. We must produce fruit. But how do we do this? By staying connected to the main source "Jesus Christ". Our profession in Christ must be genuine enough to bear fruit. We must walk and live in such a way that others will recognize that you belong to Christ, and that he lives in you so that you will be able to draw disciples to Him. This is the great commission in **Matthew 28:19 - Go ye therefore, and teach all nations, baptizing them in the name of the Father, and of the Son, and of the Holy Ghost.** You must bear fruit or Jesus will take you away. You cannot draw anyone to Christ if you are living and doing what the individual is doing. Get serious about your relationship with Christ and about completing your divine assignment in Him. You must also remember you cannot receive a reward for a production you did not do. **This is the no fruit Christian.**

Then, Jesus says every branch that bears fruit he purges it so that it will continue bearing fruit. So many things in the Christian life may not be the way the Lord wants it to be after walking with Him for a while. Such things as your thought process, behavior, attitudes, commitments, motives, passions, dedication, and many other things that should be conforming to the will of God. If these things do not conform to the purpose of producing more fruit, then God will have to prune the areas for fruit production preparation. Please note this may be a painful process but it is not meant to hurt or punish the individual. It is to remove needless spots, blemishes, or whatever needs to be removed. Just as the pruning process of a beautiful plant, this takes place to make it even more beautiful and to help it reach its fullest growth. This process may cause pain, but it returns a beauty or production that will glorify God for your next level of fruit production.

This will also move you into a closer relationship with the Lord enabling you to produce more and more fruit. This is an ongoing process, and it will happen whenever the Lord knows you need to be pruned. This is also for your good.

I often think about how much God must really love me, that he would take the time to notice the exact time in my life that I need to be pruned. Because after the pruning, I notice He will give me other assignments and I will notice new growth in my life as I prepare for His greater use. It is during this time that I really notice a closer walk with Him, and I have clearer directions as to His will for my life. Pruning is absolutely necessary if I plan to glorify God as I mature.

During your fruit bearing stages you will notice a maturing of your Spiritual Fruit. This is why fruit bearing is so very vital for your growth. As you grow, your spiritual fruit grows too. Is not this so very amazing? The pruning process is trimming away bad spots, blemishes, unwanted weight that is holding you back, and things that are not needed for your next level. **Hebrews 12:1b says let us lay aside every weight, and the sin which doth so easily beset us.** This is pruning.

When we can understand this, bearing fruit is what we will live to do.

Remember: Only you can produce the fruit that is required of you by God. So, only you can abide in Christ and allow Him to abide in you, to make you a productive vessel for the Master's use.

NOTES

Month Two - Stages of Fruit Bearing

Scripture text for reference and discussion John 15:1-5

1)-I am the true vine, and my father is the husbandman. 2)-Every
branch in me that beareth not fruit he taketh away: and every
branch that beareth fruit, he purgeth it, that it may bring forth
more fruit. 3)-Now you are clean through the word which I have
spoken unto you. 4)-Abide in me, and I in you. As the branch
cannot bear fruit of itself, except it abide in the vine; no more can
ye, except ye abide in me. 5)-I am the vine, ye are the branches: He
that abideth in me, and I in him, the same bringeth forth much
fruit: for without me ye can do nothing.

Learning and reading from this same passage of Scriptures, we will discuss the stages of fruit bearing.

There are four stages of fruit bearing mentioned in this Scripture. **They are (1) - No fruit, (2) - Fruit, (3) - More fruit, and (4) - Much fruit.**

I will start with:

Stage One - No Fruit- In this stage of fruit bearing, your spiritual tree or life have no fruit. You are saved, you know Jesus, but you are not producing any fruit. You must question why you are not bearing fruit. It is always a good thing to keep up with what is going on in your own life. Do not let much time go by without making progress. This is what I call a very dangerous stage when it comes to your spiritual productivity in Christ. You are professing Christ to others but not possessing the spiritual requirements to produce fruit.

This is the stage where the Christian (branch) is connected to the vine (Jesus), because Jesus said every branch in me that beareth not fruit He takes away. So, these Christians have a problem, they do not relate to Christ enough to become productive in fruit bearing. They stayed close enough to the vine to actually start budding as most trees do, but somehow and at some point, they do not draw enough nourishment from the vine or source to become a productive fruit bearer. They start losing their desire for the faith. There could be many reasons for the distractions, but the results are the same "No Fruit."

In their walk with the Lord, they become unattached to the things of God and become more interested in the cares of life and their own desires. When you do not stay close enough to Jesus and continue to build upon your relationship with Him, you will begin drifting away, neglecting the things of God, and leaning towards your own understanding. You may even get to the point that you will abandon the faith for the things of the world. This is why this stage is so dangerous. This is where the Scripture says, every branch in me that beareth not fruit He taketh away. Meaning, Jesus prunes or remove the unproductive branch and takes it away. This is not something you want to happen to you.

You see, every branch is responsible for making sure his profession is genuine enough to bear fruit **(Matthew 3:10 - Now also the axe is laid unto the root of the trees: therefore, every tree which bringeth not forth good fruit is hewn down and cast into the fire).** Check on your fruit because this is a severe warning to every branch (Christian) in Jesus who is not genuine enough to bear fruit.

As Christians, we are not to practice sinning. We are to practice living righteous and holy. Does this mean we will not make mistakes or even fall? No. But we are not to live as if Christ has not delivered us from the works of our flesh and fleshly desires. This is the point where every Christian must be transformed by the renewing of the mind. The mind will play a great part in your fruit production stage. We must live to please God at all costs and remember how much God hates sin. Just as God hates sin so must every Christian hate sin also (not the person), and this alone should produce a level of dedication and resistance to sin. You cannot love God and love sin too. **You must make the choice regarding how you feel about sin.**

This stage is called the unfruitful stage because the branch cannot or will not bear any fruit. Christians must always remain faithful and fruitful in Christ Jesus our Lord or there is a warning here to be taken very seriously and heeded. The Scripture states that the unfruitful branch will be taken away. So, we must be fruitful in Christ Jesus or removed.

*****This also is a Choice that each of us must make.**

Stage Two - Fruit - This stage is the first line of fruit production for the branch. The branch has begun to bring forth fruit. The fruit is now in full display and there is not mistake that this is a genuine branch or believer. The branch has stayed connected close enough to the vine to receive all the proper nutrients needed to become fruitful.

The branch (Christian) has obeyed the teachings of the Word of God, has chosen the path of righteousness over the choices of selfishness. Have allowed the Word of God to take deep root within the heart and refused to obey the lust of the flesh and the world. They have learned to hear the voice of the Lord and seek His directions for his/her life. They have determined to walk daily with the Lord, praise Him for all of His goodness, and live to bring glory to His name and His name alone. Therefore, the fruit of righteousness is now a vital part of his life.

In this stage the Christian is productive and to stay productive there is a need to be pruned. You might wonder why prune the branch if it is already producing fruit. Well, to continue producing good fruit that will remain or last, the branch must be healthy enough to reproduce forever, this is not a onetime thing. It does not matter how healthy a tree may be, there will always be imperfections in the branches because we are human.

The Lord, being the loving Vine of the branches knows the exact time that each branch needs to be pruned of spots, wrinkles, and blemishes. You may wonder what these are. Well, they are bad thoughts, bad attitudes, the need of a deeper commitment, change in behavior, unproductive relationships, and a need to give better service to the Lord. You may have passions that are against the will of God, motives that are not needed as a Christian, and many other things that may hinder a healthy production of your fruit. Fruit that are blemished will not be an acceptable production, so pruning is to keep the fruit healthy.

Pruning is absolutely necessary for the next level or stage of fruit bearing. In the pruning process, only God can give you the proper trials and testing that will produce the type and level of fruit needed for your unique personal walk and relationship with Him. Always remember you are not being punished, hurt or damaged, but pruned. There is a difference here. Your pruning will make you much better and more productive. Since you are now living to please God, only He knows what it will take to bring glory to Him. When you can recognize that the pruning is done by God with love, you will receive the process with joy and not constant complaining. Yield to the hand of God pruning you.

While you are in the pruning process continue to read and obey the words of Scripture on a daily basis, because you are cleansed by the word that Jesus has spoken unto you. Also, as you study the Word of God (Bible), you will see yourself as God begin to remove things from you that are not like Him and start conforming you into His likeness. This transformation will encourage you to go on.

As this transformation takes place in your life you will abide in Christ, and He will abide in you. You will become more persuaded to stay in Christ, to walk closer with Him, and become more and more obedient to his will for your life. You will develop the type of desire for God's presence that cannot be explained by human reasoning and words. You are growing as you submit to the will of God for you.

***Now you are ready for the next stage of fruit bearing.

Stage Three - More Fruit - After the Lord has finished pruning you in the fruit bearing stage, you are now ready to bear more fruit. Your branches are much healthier spiritually and able to bear more spiritual weight that must be carried.

You are starting to mature into the Christian you were always meant to be in Christ. You are not submitting to the old cravings of your past life, but walking more and more in the Holy Spirit and conforming to the works of the Spirit. What a great change. You are in fruit production mode now and bearing fruit is what you do. You are now able to recognize the voice of God in your life and apply whatever he is telling you, to your life so that you will experience abundant life. **What a growth spurt in your life!**

You will experience such a closeness to Christ now, because He promised in verse four of this Scripture **"Abide in me, and I in you. As the branch cannot bear fruit of itself, except it abide in the vine; no more can ye, except ye abide in me."** Your relationship with Christ is one that you are really enjoying now and looking forward to every encounter with Him. The transformation in your life is genuine and the results are fruit productivity. More fruit is what you produce now.

This should give the maturing Christian the confidence and humility needed to stick with the perfect will of God, knowing that you will continue to be productive in Him. The more fruit you bear, the more fruit you will desire to bear. You begin to desire and experience the abundant life in Christ Jesus that He promised you **(John 10:10b - I am come that they might have life, and that they might have it more abundantly).** Your more fruit bearing stage will produce abundant life in you. You will never need to look for abundant life because it is in you, and you are walking it out daily.

You will begin to recognize that after every productive season of fruit bearing, the pruning must happen to keep you more productive. Now you are ready for stage four of fruit bearing, because your branches are well kept and preserved by none other than Jesus Christ Himself. There is strength in your branches to carry fruit.

*****What an awesome blessing to know that Jesus will allow your fruit to remain.**

Stage Four - Much Fruit - In this stage the Christian (branch) has become so connected to Jesus (the vine) that he/she is praising and glorifying the Lord always. This does not mean that you are no longer experiencing testing, trials, or tribulations, but you have learned to trust God totally and recognize that God knows what is best for you. You are now willing to accept what God wants for you in your life, not what you think is best. Your will has now been placed in its proper place, behind you and God's will is all that really matters. You have learned to allow God to lead you all the way.

You are not rebelling against the will of God, but walking in the fullness of the fruit of the Spirit. You have become so caught up in the fact that God will do just what He said He would do. Therefore, you are no longer worrying about the outcome of your situations. You know the test are all for your good and not for harm. You have come to the realization that God really loves you because He is pruning you.

Your life has become so attached to Jesus and nourished by his Word and power, that you have developed and matured your spiritual fruit. Jesus your provider is supplying you with so much life-giving nutrients and now you are not just a professing Christian, you are a genuine possessing child of God. You are truly walking in the righteousness of God, and have developed godly character to the point that you are able to make disciples for the Kingdom of God.

When people see mature spiritual fruit in the lives of believers they begin to turn from the world unto Jesus. They will see and notice such a change in you that they will draw confidence that God could do the same thing for them. Sometimes people will ask questions about the God you serve just because you are a genuine Christian. Now your light is shining, and people see the change in you.

As long as the Christian is bearing much fruit, he/she will always bring glory to God. He is loving and honoring God by the life he is living and the productivity of fruit bearing. This is why it is so important that you and I know and remember the main reasons we must abide in Christ and let Him abide in us. We cannot bear fruit without the genuine connection to Jesus because He is the True Vine! He is the only sustainer of our strength and spiritual fruit. Also, that without Jesus we can do nothing. This is the connection between spiritual fruit production and maturing your spiritual fruit.

Remember: To abide in Christ means to obey, love, honor, reverence, submit to, and live in Him. Also, when you bear fruit, you show God that you are thankful that He chose you to be a part of Him and His Kingdom work!

NOTES

Month Three - Where are You in the Stages Now?

Scripture text for reference and discussion

John 15:1-5

1)-I am the true vine, and my father is the husbandman. 2)-Every
branch in me that beareth not fruit he taketh away: and every
branch that beareth fruit, he purgeth it, that it may bring forth
more fruit. 3)-Now you are clean through the word which I have
spoken unto you. 4)-Abide in me, and I in you. As the branch
cannot bear fruit of itself, except it abide in the vine; no more can
ye, except ye abide in me. 5)-I am the vine, ye are the branches: He
that abideth in me, and I in him, the same bringeth forth much
fruit: for without me ye can do nothing.

EXAMINING MYSELF!

The four stages of fruit bearing mentioned in this Scripture are: **(1) - No fruit, (2) - Fruit, (3) - More fruit, and (4) - Much fruit.** Let me personally examine my life to find the stage of fruit bearing I am walking in at this present time. I must be honest with myself so that I can get the help I need from The Almighty God.

Stage One:

No fruit - Are you the Christian who have been walking with the Lord for a while but can't seem to get out of your own way? Are you constantly complaining about what you want, when can you get it, and rebelling against the will of God? There was once an excitement in you but now it is gone. This has been going on for quite some time, but you will not seek the help you need. Now you are not interested in getting right anymore, in fact you are okay with where you are.

Remember in the previous chapter I discussed the behavior of the no fruit stage. How that the branch or Christian is in Jesus but not producing. There was a time when the branch was spouting and even budding enough to be called a branch, but what happened that stopped the productivity of the branch? Let us talk about some of the things that can cause a Christian to be in the no fruit stage.

1) - Self-denial - Are you aware of selfish behavior on your part as to not being able to do the will of God before doing what you want to do first? Scripture teaches us in **(Matthew 16:24b -If any man will come after me, let him deny himself, and take up his cross, and follow me).** Jesus knows that it is impossible to be productive and please Him if you cannot put Him first in your life. If you do not put Him first, you cannot come after Him. Knowing this fact, you will not draw the proper nutrients from the living vine that is needed to keep you living and productive. Your love for Christ must produce a self-denying attitude in you or you will always be the most important person in your life. God will not come second in your life. You can only stay in this condition for so long before it begin to draw you away from your Heavenly Father. Remember this behavior is very dangerous for a Christian because it will make you think more of yourself than you should. It is very deceiving to you but not to others. Sooner or later, you will become rebellious. Your resistance to fleshly desires is getting weaker by the day and you are finding yourself thinking more and more of these things.

2) - Rebellious - Once you are unable to deny yourself you start picking up a rebellious attitude towards the will of God. You are still professing to be a Christian, but not living up to the things of God. You may even find yourself picking up old habits that you know is totally against the life of a Christian and ignoring the voice of the Holy Spirit. Your respect for God is weak and you are okay with this. You seem to be uninterested in reading or studying the Bible, knowing this is your lifeline to God. You are moving further away from the true vine. Now instead of building up your fruit of the Spirit, you are gratifying your flesh. When you start obeying the lust and cravings of your flesh each day your resistance gets lower and lower. You are starting to become addicted to the works of your flesh, please read **(Galatians 5:19-21).** You see it is possible for a Christian to fall into this behavior if he/she keep rejecting and rebelling against the will of God.

3) - Worldliness - Now you are starting to walk, talk, and live like the world. You are craving more and more of the world and starting to feel good about it. You make excuses as to why you are doing what you do and refuse to listen to anyone who wants or try to help you. You have ignored the Holy Spirit so long until you just do not recognize His leading and guiding you anymore. The warning sign is there **"DANGER, DANGER, DANGER"** but you cannot see it anymore. Many will say you are okay but, in all reality, you know you are not.

***__Even when we become Christians, God still gives us choices.__ He wants us to love, honor, trust, and obey Him because we want to. When we decide to choose our will above the will of God, He will let us have our way. If you are in this stage of fruit bearing (no fruit), please let me remind you of the Scriptures in **(Galatians 5:24-26 - [24]-And they that are Christ's have crucified the flesh with the affections and lusts. [25]-If we live in the Spirit, let us also walk in (keep in step) the Spirit. [26]-Let us not be desirous of vain (conceited) glory, provoking one another, envying one another).**

If you find yourself heading in this direction, please stop, seek God with your whole heart, and change the direction in which you are going. Remember this is the stage where he prunes and takes the branch away. You do not want to be removed from the vine. Jesus Christ is the only true source and supply of nutrients needed for you to stay connected to Him. **There are no substitutes!**

***Are you in this stage? Do you need to be removed? You can fix what is broken.

Stage Two:

Fruit - You are now living the life of a genuine Christian. You have decided to deny yourself and walk in the perfect will of God. You still make mistakes, but you are not a practicing sinner anymore. **(Remember the Scripture in Romans 6:1-2 - [1-]What shall we say then? Shall we continue in sin, that grace may abound? [2-]God forbid. How shall we,**

that are dead to sin, live any longer therein?). There is a difference. You are taking steps towards Jesus, and you are resisting the urges to obey the cravings of your flesh. Sometimes it is hard or difficult, but you are reading the bible enough, focusing on the power of God, and not relying on your own strength. You are starting to settle into this new life and new chance you have been given in Christ Jesus.

1) - Walking By Faith - You are taking one day at a time to meet the challenges of self-denial and thanking the Lord every step of the way. Because of this you are developing more and more godly character and feeling good about the person God is transforming you into. You recognize and accept the fact that all of your sins are forgiven, you are not abiding by the laws of sin anymore but learning by faith to walk in the righteousness of God through Christ Jesus our Lord. **The Word of God in Habakkuk 2:4b - But the just shall live by his faith.**

2) - Total Surrendering to the Lord - This is making such a difference in your entire life now. Your thought process is different now because your mind is transforming into the mind of Christ **(Romans 12:2- And be not conformed to this world: but be ye transformed by the renewing of your mind, that ye may prove what is that good, and acceptable, and perfect, will of God).** You have a much better attitude because of the renewed heart. You no longer have a selfish behavior nor evil motives. Your relationship with others are flourishing because of your commitment and passion for God and His will in your life. You are willing to surrender your life to the service of the Almighty God for His glory.

3) - Availability for God's Use - You have been pruned by God but not against your will. Submission was very necessary for God to have His way in your life **(James 4:7a-Submit yourselves therefore to God).** Now that you have been pruned, you are bearing fruit in your life and fruit for the kingdom of God. You can now be used by God because you made yourself available to the Master. This process of staying connected to the true vine have made you a lively branch with the ability, by the grace of God, to bear fruit. You could not do any of this on your own. All your help comes from God. He was and is with you every step of the way, and He needed you to agree with Him to have His way in your life.

4) - Saying Yes to God - Please notice that in the stages of fruit bearing you must always make the choice to say yes to the will of God, or you will not be a productive fruit bearer **(James 4:8a-Draw nigh to God, and He will draw nigh to you).** God will not force you to serve, love, honor, praise, obey, or walk with Him against your will or desires. But He will give you the opportunity to say **YES LORD!**

***Are you in this stage? Only you will know where you are in the stages.

Stage Three:

More Fruit - Now that you have started to walk in the will of God bearing fruit, it is very important that you always remember you are to grow towards perfection (maturity). You are to never become complacent in your walk with the Lord. If this should happen in your time of spiritual growth, God will begin the pruning process **(John 15:2b- and every branch that beareth fruit, he purgeth it, that it may bring forth more fruit).** During this season in your life, it will help you if you keep in mind that God is not punishing or disciplining you. He is only removing bad spots and blemishes that will destroy your production of fruit. He must keep you walking in the righteousness of God through Christ Jesus.

1) - Studying the (Scripture) Word of God - Many people start to lose hope during this time of pruning. Their focus seems to shift to so much negative thinking. This is not the time to shift to doubt or negativity. This is the time to study the Word of Scripture **(2 Timothy 2:15-Study to show thyself approved unto God, a workman that needeth not to be ashamed, rightly dividing the Word of Truth).** Because the Scriptures are living words of God, it will begin to conform you to the perfect will of God. As God take care of the pruning you must take care of the studying of His word. Open your mind and heart to allow God to complete the work He has started in you.

2) - Allow the Word of God to Cleanse You - As you study and reflect on the pure Word of God, the power of God will start the purification process on your branch. The Lord will supply His love, grace, and mercy on the areas of need and prepare you to produce more fruit **(Psalm 119:9-Wherewithal shall a young man cleanse his way? By taking heed thereto according to thy word).** You must not only study the Word, but you must take heed (obey what it says) if you want to experience the results of the promises of God's word.

3) - Glorify God in the Way You Walk - After studying the word and allowing it to cleanse you and make you whole, it is time to glorify God by the way you live. You must walk worthy of the call of God in your life every day. You cannot pick and choose how you want to do it. The orders are given by God, and you are to carry them out. This is called walking worthy of the call of God **(Ephesians 4:1-I therefore the prisoner of the Lord, beseech you that ye walk worthy of the vocation(calling) wherewith ye are called).** Please stay the course!

4) - Increase In the Knowledge of God - While walking in the call of God it is important that you carefully pay attention to the voice of God so that you will increase in the knowledge of God. You are not a stranger to God, and to stay in His will you must know His voice. Knowing the voice of God and obeying Him will strengthen your faith and you will begin to please God **(Colossians 1:10-That ye might walk worthy of the Lord unto all pleasing, being fruitful in every good work, and increasing in the knowledge of God).** The more you learn and know of God, the closer you will walk with Him.

***This is bearing more fruit. Is this where you are? Are your fruit remaining?

Stage Four:

Much Fruit - This stage will carry you for the rest of your life in Christ. You are now a genuine, mature, and productive Christian in Christ Jesus. You are walking by faith, staying in the perfect will of God, and you have fallen in love with your Holy Father. Your heart's desire is to live to please God and love Him with all of your heart, soul, and might **(Deuteronomy 6:5-And thou shalt love the Lord thy God with all thine heart, and with all thy soul, and with all thy might).** Not only are you living like this, but you are truly enjoying your walk with Christ.

1) - Your Mind have Developed into the Mind of Christ - You have developed and matured a selfless attitude, willing to sacrifice for the good of others. You have learned to walk humbly before the Lord in the spirit of love. You understand why your will is not the best thing for you, and you trust God to have His way in your life. Your mind has completely shifted to wanting and needing to please God in everything you do. What a transformed mind **(Philippians 2:5-Let this mind be in you, which was also in Christ Jesus).** Jesus always had a mind to please His Heavenly Father. Now you are living to please your heavenly Father.

2) - You are Living a Life of Righteousness - You are no longer thinking about sinning. You know now, without a doubt, that you are the righteousness of God through Christ Jesus (Romans 3:22-Even the righteousness of God which is by faith of Jesus Christ unto all and upon all of them that believe: for there is no difference). You really understand how this happened and how to inform others of this great gift of God. Because of what Christ did for you, you are now persuaded in your own heart and mind that you must share this knowledge with others.

3) - Godly Character is Matured and Others See it - You are now walking in your mature godly character, and it is being seen by others. You do not have to broadcast this to anyone because your light is shinning **(Matthew 5:14-Ye are the light of the world, a city that is set on a hill cannot be hid).** When godly character is present in the Christian's life, living holy and walking in the mature fruit of the Spirit is what you do.

Because your fruit is now mature, it will remain!

NOTES

***It is time for Spiritual Fruit Maturing!**

It is time to learn how to mature the fruit of the Spirit in your life, so that you will not walk after the lusts and desires of your flesh. As the fruit mature you will become more and more like Jesus Christ your Redeemer, Lord, and Savior.

Scripture For Reference

Galatians 5:22-23

[22)-]But the fruit of the Spirit is love, joy, peace, longsuffering, gentleness, goodness, faith, [23)-]Meekness, temperance: against such there is no law.

These are the Scriptures I will be using as the foundational structure for maturing the Fruit of the Spirit. I will work on one particular fruit at a time so you can get the full meaning on how to mature each one. This is one fruit but divided into the many traits of the Holy Spirit.

We will work on each trait for one month in increments of five days per lesson. This should give the individual proper time to learn about that fruit and how to start the maturing process.

Each session should leave the individual with substance needed for growth. It is important to note that the fruit of the Spirit is one fruit, and it comes as a gift from God, in the person of the Holy Spirit. It is the character or nature of God. This is why it is so important that all Christians understand the need to desire to mature the fruit, and become like God the Father, God the Son, and God the Holy Spirit.

We will also see why and how your production of fruit and your spiritual fruit maturity works hand together.

Let us take this journey to Spiritual Fruit Maturing!

Month Four - Maturing the Fruit of Love

Days 1 - 5

Loving God

Scripture Text

1 Corinthians 13:1-8a; 13

**1)-Though I speak with the tongues of men and of angels, and have
not charity(love), I am become as sounding brass, or a tinkling
cymbal. 2)-And though I have the gift of prophecy, and understand
all mysteries, and all knowledge; and though I have faith, so that
I could remove mountains, and have not charity, I am nothing.
3)-And though I bestow all my goods to feed the poor, and though
I give my body to be burned, and have not charity, it profiteth me
nothing. 4)-Charity suffereth long, and is kind; charity envieth not;
charity vaunteth not itself, is not puffed up, 5)-Doth not behave
itself unseemly, seeketh not her own, is not easily provoked,
thinketh no evil; 6)-Rejoiceth not in iniquity, but rejoiceth in the
truth; 7)-Beareth all things, believeth all things, hopeth all things,
endureth all things. 8a)-Charity never faileth. 13)-And now abideth
faith, hope, charity, these three; but the greatest of these is charity.**

This passage of Scripture is so important because it teaches all of us as Christians how great, powerful, humbling, and needful it is to house the fruit of love deep in our hearts. This Scripture comes after the powerful teaching on spiritual gifts that are given by the Holy Spirit to every believer. The Spiritual gifts are very powerful because they come from our powerful God. Paul the writer realized that the more perfect way to utilize the gifts would be in the power of love.

He wanted the Corinthian Church to know that it did not matter how great their gifts were, if the receiver of the gift did not understand the power of operating in the spiritual fruit of LOVE given by God, they have done nothing. Paul's tone of speech was heavy, because he wanted everyone to get the proper understanding, to not work their gift if it was not worked in love. He wanted them to know that it did not matter how extreme their giving was, how beautiful their voices may sound, how many poor people they fed, how much knowledge they had obtained, or how popular they were, if love was not the real motive behind their doings, it was useless.

1) - The first step to maturing the spiritual gift of love would be, to understand how deep the love of God is and how deep the Christian's love should be. You may say I will never be able to love on that level, but I will say to you God knows this. He expects you and I to come as close to the mark as possible. God knows that as time is given by the believers to study and understand the nature and character of God, love will begin to blossom inside of you. The Holy Spirit will help you in this area. This is one of the purpose the Holy Spirit was sent.

God loves us so much that He gave His only begotten Son to die for our sins because He knew we would never accomplish righteousness on our own. We all were enemies of God. While we were actively sinning, God sent Jesus to die a horrible death of crucifixion just for us to become friends and sons of God. This was not done for just one group of people but for everyone who will accept it **(John 3:16-For God so loved the world, that He gave his only begotten Son, that whosoever believeth in Him should not perish, but have everlasting life).**

2) - This is who God is. This is What He does. This is agape love, the love of God's mind, His will, and His reason. God thinks in love, He feels in love, He operates in love. Everything God does is motivated by and in His love. To paint a picture of God would be to paint pure love on a canvas, because this is who God is! He loves us even when we are unlovable, when we do not deserve to be loved, and if we do not feel like He should love us. He loves us still.

People who hate God, rejects Him, refuse to serve Him, and do not believe that He exists, God still loves them, because this is who He is.

This is the love that we should be striving to achieve as our walk with the Lord matures. This is how men will know that you belong to God, by the love that radiates in, through, and from you. If everything else in your life fails or fall apart, you can have confidence that God's love for you will never fail. His love remains the same because **God is Unchanging!**

The love of God will suffer long, and it is kind. His love is not jealous of others and does not parade itself. God's love is not arrogant and does not behave itself unseemly, it is not selfish, and not easily provoked. The love of God does not think evil of others. True love does not rejoice in wrong doings, but rejoices in the truth. The pure love of God bears all things, believes all things, hope all things, and endures all things. This is why God's love will never fail. This is the truth of God's love for all mankind. We should practice daily to mimic this same type of love in our Christian walk. We are to be just like Jesus every day.

3) - The Christian's love can mature if the proper time is spent in living, talking, obeying, and trusting the Holy Spirit to have His way in his/her life daily (1 Corinthians 13: 8a - Charity never faileth). Spend these five days reading, studying, and changing your mind about loving people who you feel is so hard to get along with. Do not make any excuses as to why you cannot do it, but make a conscious decision that you will love the way God requires you to love.

During these days think about some of the relationships you have walked away from. People who were so important to you, but you allowed matters to destroy those relationships. Look into your fruit of love and see what you could have done differently or could do now to fix it. Do not think about what the person could do to make this relationship better, but how this would help to mature your spiritual fruit of love. Even if the person did not give the love that you needed to keep the relationship going, consider what would it take on your part to work it out.

***This week look deep within your heart to see whether selfishness or pride played a part of your inability to mature your love in this matter. Work on this from your heart.

Remember, that the first step to maturing your spiritual fruit of love is to love the Lord with all your heart (Deuteronomy 6:5- And thou shalt love the Lord thy God with all thine heart, and with all thy soul, and with all thy might).

Days 6 - 10

Loving One Another

Scripture Text

John 13:34-25

34)-A new commandment I give unto you, that ye love one another; as I have loved you, that you also love one another. 35)-By this shall all men know that ye are my disciples, if ye have love one to another.

In this particular Scripture Jesus was getting ready to face crucifixion and He realized that His disciples would not see His presence anymore. He needed to give them the assurance that He would still be with them in Spirit. He gave them a new commandment to love one another the same way that He had loved them.

Jesus knew His disciples had issues in the area of love and a struggle for earthly power. He knew all of these things about each of them, but Jesus still wanted to use them to spread His Gospel. Therefore, He commanded them to love one another because He understood the power of love. Jesus also knew that the only way they would be able to live and walk in this type of love He is commanding, would be through the indwelling of His Holy Spirit. Always know that the Lord will never ask any of us to do anything that we cannot perform. This is the reason He sent the Holy Spirit, fully equipped with the fruit of the Spirit, to abide in us and we abide in Him.

Jesus knew each disciple was different, had different behaviors, thought differently, and did things differently. They had to be filled with the pure love of God to work together, to accomplish the divine will of God in the earth. They could not get anything done if they did not love and respect each other. They had walked with Jesus and experienced the way He truly loved and cared for them **(John 13:34 - A new commandment I**

give unto you, that ye love one another; as I have loved you, that you also love one another). They had to learn to love!

Jesus taught them by example and teachings **(Matthew 5:2-And He opened His mouth and taught them saying).** Now he was sending them out to do the same things. Just as Jesus had obeyed His Father, now He was sending His Spirit back to empower them to carry out His work. The disciples learned love and obedience from Jesus, but they could not walk it out without the power of the Holy Spirit. Jesus told His disciples to go down to Jerusalem and stay there until He give them some power to carry out their assignments **(Acts 1:8a - But ye shall receive power, after that the Holy Ghost is come upon you).**

1) - The same applies to you and I also. We cannot love the way God commands without the presence of His Spirit. The love of God comes from God because it is His love. There is no other way you can love with the love of God, without having him abiding inside of you. This is not the normal physical love, it is the love of God's Spirit that He places in the Christian's heart **(John 15:12-This is my commandment, that ye love one another, as I have loved you).** Just as Jesus drew His disciples to Himself, the Holy Spirit will draw others to God through the believers love for Him and each other. This type of love is very powerful!

2) - This is a love that cannot be walked out through pretending. It must be true love, because Jesus is the truth and His love is true and offered to all that will accept it **(John 14:6 - Jesus saith unto him, I am the way, the truth, and the life: no man cometh unto the Father, but by me).** This may sound like something very difficult to accomplish, truthfully in your own power it is impossible. That is why Jesus sent His Holy Spirit to reside within each of us Christians to make this love happen.

When Believers in Christ can love one another from their heart and get along with each other, the role of making disciples for Christ will be what we do. We all have a divine assignment that we must complete in

Christ, but if we cannot get along with and love one another as Christ loves us, our living will be in vain.

***The second step to maturing our spiritual fruit of love, would be to learn how to love one another as commanded by Jesus Christ our Lord!

Remember, take the time to change your mind about the way you desire to love others and practice putting other peoples' feeling above your own. This will help you fight the urge to be selfish and only concerned about you.

Days 11 - 15
Walking in Forgiveness
Scripture Text
Matthew 6:12, 14-15

12)-And forgive us our debts, as we forgive our debtors. 14)-For if ye forgive men their trespasses, your heavenly Father will also forgive you: 15)-But if ye forgive not men their trespasses, neither will your Father forgive your trespasses.

In these Scriptures, Jesus' disciples had asked Him to teach them how to pray. Jesus responded by telling them the things they should include in their prayer to His Father. He comes to this particular point where He tells them to ask His Heavenly Father to forgive them of their debts, as they forgive others of the debt that is owed unto them. That is so powerful in itself because, Jesus is teaching them to ask for forgiveness as they are willing to forgive others. If you forgive much, then you love much. If you forgive little, then you love little. It is that simple because love covers a multitude of sins **(1 Peter 4:8-And above all things have fervent charity (love) among yourselves: for charity (love) shall cover the multitude of sins).** True love will forgive over and over, it will not keep count or scores!

This along will show how much you are willing to love. How much you are willing to let go of things to love the way God calls you to love. Can you let it go for the sake of keeping love pure? This is where so many Christians start to struggle in the area of loving others as Christ have loved them.

1) - Forgiving is an act of love. If you can forgive someone who wronged you, then your love for them is greater than the things they did to you. It makes you realize that they are human just as you are. You will begin to see how much we all even as Christians, need the empowerment of the Holy Spirit to keep us on the straight and narrow path of Gods' righteousness.

Following these steps of forgiveness will truly mature your spiritual fruit of love. Forgiving others will teach you how to walk in the Spirit and not after the flesh. Your fleshly behavior will tell you to get rid of the person, but the Holy Spirit will keep telling you to forgive and let it go. You will begin to mature especially when you recognize that they are needed in the body of Christ to fulfill their part in the work of the ministry, as called of God.

2) - Another way of seeing it is, to realize that maybe the Lord placed that person in the body to help you mature in the areas of need. So, embrace them and grow your fruit of love. Do not spend so much time on complaining about the situation, apply your energy to forgive and grow. Also remember you cannot change someone else, but you can change you. God has given you the power to change your mind not someone else's mind **(Romans 12:2a - And be not conformed to this world: but be ye transformed by the renewing of your mind).**

3) - Love is more about loving people where they are and not trying to make them the way you want them to be, so that you can love them (1 John 4:11 - Beloved, if God so loved us, we ought also to love one another). Come up to the higher levels of love and love them as they are. This is real love as commanded of God. Jesus loved us while we were yet sinners. He hated the sin that held us in bondage, but he loved us and still does. Can we not see how much love is connected to the way we forgive others? These are matters of your heart.

***This is the third step to maturing your spiritual fruit of love, walking in forgiveness. Can you do this for your spiritual love fruit growth? Deal with all the matters of your heart whether they are good or bad.

Remember, as we spend this week learning about the connection between love and forgiveness, let us work on fixing broken

relationships that just need someone to make the first step towards forgiving the problem. Make this a priority so that you can start more maturing of your spiritual fruit of LOVE!

Days 16 - 20
Walking in Obedience
Scripture Text
1 John 5:2-3

2)-By this we know that we love the children of God, when we love God, and keep His commandments. 3)-For this is the love of God, that we keep His commandments: and His commandments are not grievous.

We see in these Scriptures, that to love God is to obey what He commands us to do. When we love the people of God, we show that we love Him because we cannot see God, but we can see each other. To love God is to obey Him. You cannot say you love the Lord and constantly disobey what He tells you to do. Think about it, if you are always doing the things that God tell you not to do, is this showing respect to Him? If you disrespect Him through disobedience, how can you call it love?

Jesus proved His love to God His Father by obeying everything He was sent and told to do. Jesus constantly said, "I came to do the will of Him who sent me" or "I came to do the will of my Father". Jesus understood the importance of obedience. He knew how much He loved and respected His Father so obedience would be the proof of that love. Jesus walked in total obedience to His Heavenly Father. Show how your level of obedience proves how much you love God, by doing what He said **(John 14:15 - If you love me, keep my commandments).**

1) - As Christians, we are to give glory, honor, respect, praise, and thanks to God at all times in obedience (Romans 6:17b - But ye have obeyed from the heart that form of doctrine which was delivered you). Think about this, if you brought glory to God you must live in obedience to His will. To honor God would be to walk in obedience to the things He desires from you. To respect God would be to obey Him as your Heavenly Father. To praise and thank Him would be to present yourself in obedience to Him and Him along. To walk in this level of obedience you must love God from your heart, and it must be pure and true love.

True love for God the Father, Son, and Holy Spirit would teach us the true meaning of obedience, and why it is so important to walk in obedience to God. Many times, we do not experience the fullness of the will of God because we will not walk in the fullness of obedience to Him. As you walk in obedience to God's word and His will for your life, you will find yourself experiencing such a closeness to the heart of God. You will draw sustaining nutrients from God, which will enable you to produce major growth in your spiritual fruit of love.

2) - Obedience to God is needed to grow and groom your spiritual fruit of love. Your level of love will begin to increase, because obedience will be actively promoting growth in your love fruit as you seek to please God. Obedience to God is better than anything you can give Him **(1 Samuel 15:22b - Behold, to obey is better than sacrifice, and to hearken than the fat of rams).**

3) - Loving God and obeying Him should be inseparable because they both are needed to mature your spiritual fruit of love. You cannot show the love of God without walking in the obedience God commands of you. It is His will that you learn obedience even if it is taught through the test and trials of life. Just as His Son, Jesus, learned obedience by the things He suffered, you are to do the same thing **(Hebrews 5:8-9 - [8)-]Though He were a Son yet learned He obedience by the things which He suffered, [9)-]And being made perfect, He became the author of eternal salvation unto all of them that obey Him).** Testing brings us to a place of maturity in the spiritual fruit of love.

***This is the fourth step. Walk in obedience to mature your spiritual fruit of love. Start obeying in all things, it will profit you.

Remember, how many times have you been tested in areas of obedience, and you failed to endure the test? You yielded to the cravings of your will and prayed that you would do better the next time. Take this week to study the Scriptures on obedience and purpose to practice walking in love to please God. You will be able to see that obedience will play a vital part in maturing your spiritual fruit of love.

Days 21 - 25
Walking in Humility
Scripture Text
Matthew 18:4

Whosoever therefore shall humble himself as this little child, the same is greatest in the kingdom of heaven.

Jesus had many opportunities to teach and instruct His disciples on how to get into the kingdom of heaven. He taught them about many requirements that would need to change in their life to walk in His authority. Jesus would often use visual examples to get His point across to them, to make sure they truly understood His teachings.

In this particular Scripture text Jesus was teaching them a lesson in humility. His disciples came to Him saying, who is the greatest in the kingdom of heaven? Even after walking with Jesus for a while, they still did not understand that the kingdom of heaven does not operate like the earthly kingdoms. They were looking for great positions in Jesus' kingdom, but Jesus had to set the record straight to make sure they understood what He came to this earth to do. They also needed to understand that humility is what Jesus required from them to be His disciples. They were not to seek after worldly greatness but to walk as little children desiring the will of God in their lives.

Jesus called a young child unto Him and set the child in the midst of them and began the teaching session. He told them, to be the greatest in the kingdom of heaven, they must humble (not arrogant or prideful) themselves just as the little child He set in their midst. I am sure they were quite surprised to hear such a command coming from the mouth of Jesus. After all is not, He the Son of God and He is telling them to follow Him as a child! This is exactly the point Jesus meant for them to get, they are His little children.

Early in their walk with Jesus, He expected them to change their minds from the way they thought, felt, and did things before the call to follow Him. Jesus needed them to see that they were walking out of one way of living into a new way of life. Therefore, they must start changing their perceptions on how they viewed the call of God. They needed this to happen early so they would not miss any lessons during their training. They were being trained for duty and not positions. WOW!

1) - Humility is a vital part of maturing your spiritual love fruit. It is very difficult to love someone when you are prideful and arrogant, thinking you are better than they are. When you respect, fear, and love God, this type of behavior should not be present in a Christian's life, it becomes hard to work with the individual **(Proverbs 15:33 - The fear of the Lord is the instruction of wisdom; and before honour is humility).** It is not impossible to do but it does strain the relationship. True love enables you to not think highly of yourself, but to think soberly and see the will of God for His Church and others. Pride can cause you to think you are more superior to others and you are not.

When Christians walk in pride, it displays that immaturity is present in their spiritual walk. Pruning by God is needed to mature the fruit of love. Pride is dangerous and it will bring a man very low, especially if he/she is a Christian **(Proverbs 29:23 - A man's pride shall bring him low: but honour shall uphold the humble in spirit).** Please do not let your pride keep you from maturing your love in Christ.

2) - Many times, we want to be exalted before the timing of God, this is not good. If you truly love God and trust His will and timing for your life, you will know and accept when God is ready to exalt you **(1Peter 5:5b-6 - 5b)-be clothed with humility: for God resisteth the proud and giveth grace to the humble. 6)-Humble yourselves therefore under the mighty hand of God, that He may exalt you in due time). DO NOT TRY TO GET AHEAD OF GOD, WAIT FOR HIS TIME!**

We see Jesus coming to this earth with a purpose in life. He came to redeem mankind back to His Father because we needed salvation. He humbled Himself to die on the cross for all of us. Never complaining but always doing the will of God. He did not get honor or praise from the people He came to redeem. Being treated harshly all during His earthly ministry, he was not exalted to His rightful place until He completed the task He was sent to do **(Philippians 2:8 - And being found in fashion as a man, he humbled Himself, and became obedient unto death, even the death of the cross).** This all happened in His Father's timing. You and I are no different, we must wait for God to exalt us when He is ready. I know the flesh will war against the will of God in the area of humility, but as you mature in love this will become who you are and what you do because you love God!

3) - As we walk in humility the way God requires us to do, we will see great changes in the way we love and respect others (Matthew 23:12 - And whosoever shall exalt himself shall be abased; and he that shall humble himself shall be exalted). This will also mature your spiritual fruit of love to a point that you will understand why humility is so vitally important for your spiritual love to mature. Jesus loves us so much that He wants to exalt us, but we must understand that certain changes will produce certain results. Humility produces exaltation by God, only God can give you true exaltation. Only He knows what you were meant to do.

***This is the fifth step, walking in humility. Do not allow pride to cripple the growth of your spiritual love fruit.

Remember, take this week to look into your heart to identify any pride that may be hiding and preventing your spiritual fruit of love from maturing. Your heart can hide many things that can hinder your maturity in Christ. Please work on this now!

Days 26 - 30

You Must Always Submit Your Ways unto the Lord

Scripture Text

James 4:8a

Submit yourselves therefore to God:

Realizing that the fruit of love must mature properly, it is very important that you submit yourself unto God for his continual oversight of the growth production of love. To submit means to yield or surrender your ways into the hand of God, trusting that He will supply all the necessary nutrients that you will need to become mature and to endure. You must continue in this process; you cannot start and stop.

Remember this is something you must do daily because it is your new way of life. It will take you cooperating with the Holy Spirit to make the submission happen. When you commit your development into God's care, He will establish you in whatever He has called you to do **(Proverbs 16:3 - Commit thy works unto the Lord, and thy thoughts shall be established).** You will not be required to work through this on your own. Jesus promised to never leave us, that He will be with us until the end of the world.

In maturing your spiritual fruit of love, we have learned that:

1) - Loving God with all your heart will teach you the importance of love in action. To be able to love God from your heart will show others that you are a real Christian. You will not have to tell them because they will recognize it by the way you live **(Psalm 37:5 - Commit thy way unto the Lord; trust also in Him; and He shall bring it to pass).** The way you live will give others the permission to do the same thing.

2) - The active display of genuine love for God will produce the action of loving one another from your heart. It is hard to love others without the presence and abiding help of the Holy Spirit. Since the Holy Spirit lives inside of you, the power of love is present inside of you also, because God is love. The love of God will soften the hard places in your heart and love will flow from your heart to others.

Loving one another will prohibit so much stumbling alone your walk as a Christian and will show others how to love because you are now walking in the light **(1 John 2:10 - He that loveth his brother abideth in the light, and there is none occasion of stumbling in him).** Keep walking in the light of God's will for you.

3) - When you start loving one another from the heart, you will start walking in forgiveness. It is impossible to truly love someone without being able and committed to forgiving them. All of this works together. Love and forgiveness are needed to make the fruit mature. This will help to remove selfishness out of your heart and replace it with love. Forgiving others will allow God to erase your debts also **(Matthew 15 - But if ye forgive not men their trespasses; neither will your Father forgive your trespasses).** Do not hold debt on others if you do not want debt held over you!

4) - As your love begin to mature, you will find yourself walking in obedience to the will of God. You are no longer consumed with having your way all the time. Now you are concerned about the things of God and others. Sometimes you may not notice that you have changed but someone else will see the difference. You must bring everything about you under the obedience of God's rule and daily walk-in obedience **(2 Corinthians 10:5 - Casting down imaginations, and every high thing that exalteth itself against the knowledge of God and bringing into captivity every thought to the obedience of Christ).**

5) - As obedience is active in your life, humility begin to spring fourth because you are no longer rebelling against the will of God.

The love of God is so powerful that it grooms, softens, and prepares the heart to produce love on a level you never thought possible. This type and level of love brings God's abundant life into action in your life **(John 10:10b - I am come that they might have life, and that they might have it more abundantly).**

***So now in week six, you should be ready to submit yourself and all of your ways unto the Lord. The love of God will prompt you to walk in such a way that you will desire to please Him, because love is what you do!

1) - This is where you commit to studying the word of God daily, to continue the growth process and to show yourself approved unto Him. Do not just read the bible but commit to studying and searching for the truth **(2 Timothy 2:15 - Study to shew thyself approved unto God, a workman that needeth not to be ashamed, rightly dividing the word of truth).**

2) - You must also commit to praying always without ceasing (to put to an end or to discontinue). It is not a good practice to pray only when you feel like it or when you need something from God. You must learn to pray always and keep in constant communication with Him. **PRAYER** is how you do this. Just as you and I keep in contact with others through talking, so must you do the same with God. This is the way you learn his voice and how you get instructions on how to live for Him. Loving God is communicating with Him too. Do not rely on others to communicate with God for you all the time, do this for yourself **(1 Thessalonians 5:17 - Pray without ceasing).**

3) - Commit to Acknowledging God in all you do. Get into the habit of consulting God before making decisions, not after the fact. When we fail to seek God's approval in matters, we tend to make many errors. This can pull you off of your dependence on God and pride can set in. As long as you know you need God and include Him in all of your ways, He will direct your path. Your spiritual fruit of love can only grow, and you will be able to love the way God requires of you **(Proverbs 3:5-6 - 5)-Trust in the Lord with all thine heart; and lean not unto thine own understanding.6)-In all thy ways acknowledge Him, and He shall direct thy path).**

*****With completion of this month trust God and see "Your Spiritual Fruit of Love Mature".**

NOTES

Month Five - Maturing the Fruit of Joy

Days 1 - 5
Joy In Serving God
Scripture Text
John 15:11

These things have I spoken unto you, that my Joy might remain in you, and that your joy might be full.

In this passage of Scripture, Jesus is talking to his disciples about abiding in Him as He abides in His Father. He is getting ready to die for the sins of the world and did not want them to feel like there was no hope after He went back to His Father in heaven. It was Jesus desired for them to stay connected to Him (the vine) so that they would always have JOY and not despair. Jesus already knew everything that would happen to them, and He did not want them to feel all alone, because He loved them. Jesus wanted the disciples to have pure joy in their hearts.

While Jesus was walking with them, they had joy because they could see Him, they could touch Him, and whatever they needed to learn, all they had to do was ask Jesus. The day was fast approaching when their joy would be tested because they would no longer physically see Him or be in His presence to touch Him. The disciples always depended on Jesus leading and teaching them in all things. For Jesus to leave them, what would they experience as His disciples, not knowing what to expect next.

Jesus knew that he needed to prepare His disciples for the test of His crucifixion, by informing them that He desired their joy to be full and remain in them. This is very important information Jesus is giving them because they needed to have joy in serving the Lord. They would need some spiritual help and power. This would only happen if Jesus went back to Heaven to be with God the Father and send His Holy Spirit back to live inside of them **(John 14:16 - And I will pray the Father, and He shall**

give you another Comforter, that He may abide with you forever).

Jesus was not worried about His disciples not having Joy, because He knew the true source of where joy comes from and how it would remain in them. Jesus knew what to do, whom to send, and how to give it to His twelve servants. The plan was already activated and ready to be implemented at the appointed time.

1) - Scripture teaches us that the joy of the Lord is our strength (Nehemiah 8:10c - For the joy of the Lord is your strength). For the disciples to be productive in starting "The New Testament Church", they needed the strength that comes from **Spiritual Joy.** Being happy would not give them the strength and power they needed for the charge they would be given, by Jesus, to be carried out.

2) - Jesus' joy came from serving and obeying His father. He constantly stated that He came to do the will of His Father (John 4:34 - Jesus saith unto them, my meat is to do the will of him that sent me, and to finish his work). He kept His mind on doing what He was sent to do and did not let things or people distract Him. He understood His mission and knew the only way to please God the Father, was to finish what He came to do. The disciples needed this same joy to succeed.

3) - Joy is such an awesome fruit of the Spirit. Joy is an inner gladness; a deep-seated pleasure in the heart that gives you a cheerful behavior even in the midst of trouble. Joy is deep assurance and confidence that makes the heart cheerful. It is not governed by circumstances and cannot be obtained without God. Joy is not like happiness. Circumstances produces happiness, but the Holy spirit gives you joy. This is the reason it is so important to mature your spiritual fruit of joy.

The Holy Spirit lives inside of the Christian, therefore the fruit of joy is in the heart of the believer. As the individual matures spiritually, so must his/her fruit of joy mature. Joy can only be obtained through the indwelling of the Holy Spirit. It is called a spiritual fruit because it comes from the Spirit of God. It cannot be obtained any other way. Please do not mistake joy for happiness. Many people make this mistake. Happiness is measured by circumstances and is temporary, but joy comes from God and is permanent! Wouldn't you rather have joy?

When you become a servant of the Most High God, and receive the gift of the Holy Spirit, the spiritual fruit of joy is included. Being that the Holy Spirit is the Spirit of God, He does not change when your circumstances change. **His joy is still present and available to the Christian for usage at all times (John 15:11 - These things have I spoken unto you, that, my joy might remain in you, and that your joy might be full).** There is true joy in serving God, and as you walk with Him your fruit of joy should walk and grow with you.

4) - **As a Christian serving God should be a joy, a gladness of heart, and a deep pleasure because you were delivered from the bondage of sin and shame.** You are now reconnected back to God, and given His spirit to serve Him. You have been given a spiritual charge to carry His gospel to the entire universe, this alone should bring deep seated joy into your heart. Do not spend time looking for happiness, seek for the joy of God in your life.

***During these first five days rekindle the fire and flames in your service for the Lord. Allow the Holy Spirit to release the joy that you once knew so well.

Remember, start by studying the Scriptures and making yourself available to hear from and be used by the Almighty God. This is week one of maturing your spiritual fruit of JOY!

Days 6 - 10

Where Does Joy Come from?

Scripture Text

John 16:22-23

**22)-And ye now therefore have sorrow: but I will see you again,
and your heart shall rejoice, and your joy no man taketh from
you. 23)-And in that day ye shall ask me nothing. Verily, verily, I
say unto you, Whatsoever ye shall ask the Father in my name, He
will give it you.**

In these Scriptures, Jesus is giving His farewell to His twelve disciples. He is letting them know that things will be very different for them from now on. They will have to approach Him in a different manner, but the results will be the same. They would not be left to make it on their own, but they will go to God the Father in the name of Jesus. Jesus told them that they would have sorrow when He leave them, but it will only last shortly. Jesus promised that he will see them again and the joy they will experience can never be taken away from them.

Jesus gave them hope for the future! He gave them the promise of better days. They were being told that Jesus mission was ending, and their mission was just starting. Jesus would no longer be their teacher and master, but he would now become their Lord, Savior, Redeemer, Mediator, and King! This would be the foundation of their joy.

The joy that Jesus promised them would not be controlled by humans but by Him. No one would have the power to give them this type of joy, and no one could take their joy away. You may option to not walk in your joy, but no one else has the power to take your joy from you. **This joy is God's gift in the Holy Spirit to you, cherish your gift. Live in your JOY daily!**

The way Jesus walked with them would be different now. Instead of them seeing Him, they now had to have faith to know that His Spirit will live inside of their hearts. So now Jesus would be even closer to them because He is walking and living inside of them. They will have the opportunity to get to know His Heavenly Father by using the name of Jesus to ask for anything.

1) - Joy comes from the Spirit of God (Galatians 5:22a - But the fruit of the Spirit is love, joy). That is why no one will be able to take it from you. As the Spirit of Christ abide in you and you abide in Him you will have joy. Now you must allow the Holy Spirit to have His way in your life, and trust the Spirit of Christ to grow your fruit by believing the testimony of Scriptures, regarding Jesus the Son of God. This is the reason you do not get distracted by what others say or do. If you allow the Holy Spirit to lead you, He will keep you in the joy of the Lord. Please work on Staying focused daily!

2) - Joy is divine meaning, it can only come from God (Romans 15:13 - Now the God of hope fill you with all joy and peace in believing, that ye may abound in hope, through the power of the Holy Ghost). Just as the disciples of Christ had to trust the words of Jesus, so must you and me. The God of hope fills us with His joy so that we will keep walking in hope. Joy in Christ have a way of keeping you calm and focused to complete the service of God. Keep your joy by staying in your lane and completing your assignments given to you by God!

3) - Joy comes from knowing that others are walking in the truth (3 John 1:4 - I have no greater joy than to hear that my children walk in truth). As your fruit of joy matures, you will find yourself full of joy when you hear of others walking in the truth of God's word. You start living the truth and walking by faith, with the hope of eternal life.

Joy is not selfish because of who it comes from. Just as Jesus rejoiced over His assignment to die for the sin of the world, and is now sitting on the right hand of God the Father, we must also have joy when we see others coming to Christ. This is a true sign of a mature fruit of joy. Christians must not walk in jealousy but in joy. Joy in other's accomplishments will give you more joy.

4) -Joy comes from completing the will of God (Acts 20:24 - But none of these things move me, neither count I my life dear unto myself, so that I might finish my course with joy, and the ministry, which I have received of the Lord Jesus, to testify the gospel of the grace of God). The apostle Paul was convinced that he would let nothing prevent him from completing the work and ministry of God in joy. He started it in joy, and he expected to finish it in joy. When you complete the assignments of God in your life, it brings you joy, confidence, assurance, and satisfaction in knowing Jesus. You have joy deep in your heart because He is always present to see you through the entire process.

***Now that you know where joy comes from, take this entire week to rejoice in the Lord for making His deposit of joy in your heart.

Remember, keep studying Scriptures on joy to mature what has been deposited in you.

Days 11 - 15
Walking in Joy
Scripture Text
Psalm 89:15-16

15)-Blessed is the people that know the joyful sound: They shall walk O Lord, in the light of thy countenance. 16)-In thy name shall they rejoice all the day: And in thy righteousness shall they be exalted.

This passage of Scripture from Psalm is a celebration of God's love and faithfulness to His people. It is a joyful sound to the hearing to know that you are loved by God and that He is faithful to His promises. When looking back at the promises God made to His people and how He kept His word to them, you should find confidence and assurance that your God will do the very same for you. Because of this you should find yourself walking in joy day after day.

The Christian who knows the joyful sound of God's faithfulness is called blessed (the object of God's favors). They shall walk in the leadership of God's directions and are guided by His light. Christians are to rejoice in the name of their God all day long because of who He is and what He does for His people. There is never a need or a challenge that your God cannot conquer for you. With this knowledge your joy should be full. Everyday should be a day for rejoicing in Him.

Walking in the powerful loving kindness and faithfulness of God should bring continual joy in your life. Because you walk in Christ Jesus and have made God your King, you become the recipient of God's great joy. You know that you are not the producer of your own righteousness, but it comes from God through Christ Jesus. Therefore, you are exalted into His righteousness and protected by Him constantly. What a reason to have joy unspeakable and full of glory, in your God.

1) - To walk in joy is to accept God's word to cast all of your cares upon Him because He cares for you (1 Peter 5:7 - Casting all your cares upon Him; for He careth for you). It is important to know that you serve the Almighty God who created you and is able to take great care of you every day. Therefore, you do not have to worry about what tomorrow may bring into your life. God wants you to experience what life has to offer when you can totally trust him from your heart. Yes, the cares of life can be challenging, but the love God has for you will keep you walking in joy. You must trust and allow Him to have His way in your entire life. God wants all of you, nothing else will do. Do not substitute your will for His will in your life, only He knows what is best for you.

2) - Fellowshipping with God the Father and His Son Jesus Christ will give you all the joy you need to walk daily in life (1 John1:3b-4 - [3b)-]And truly our fellowship is with the Father, and with His Son, Jesus Christ. [4)-]And these things write we unto you, that your joy may be full). As you study, receive the word of God by faith, and allow it to get rooted deep within your heart, the fruit of joy will begin to get full. The nutrients you get from the Word of God has the power to make you completely whole and mature in Christ Jesus. Stay in His word constantly!

Jesus is the Word and the more you eat the Word the more strength you will gain in Christ. Remember more Word more strength, less Word less strength. Study, study, study!

3) - Faithfulness in obeying God will bring you into the joy of the Lord (Matthew 25:21 - His lord said unto him, Well done, thou good and faithful servant: thou hast been faithful over a few things, I will make thee ruler over many things: enter thou into the joy of thy lord). As you walk before God, stay faithful and obedient in His will for you. The more you obey from your heart, the more faithful and obedient you become. Walking in the will of God daily gives you joy that you cannot understand. Even when things are not going well for you, you will still have joy. When people fail you, misunderstand, or hurt you, joy will still be your comfort.

***This is when you will know that your joy is maturing. Circumstances will no longer dictate how you walk before your God. You will rise up early in the morning with joy and lay down at night with joy.

Remember, maturity of your joy fruit is happening now!

Days 16 - 20

Hope in Christ Jesus Brings Joy

Scripture Text

Romans 15:13

Now the God of hope fill you with all joy and peace in believing, that ye may abound in hope, through the power of the Holy Ghost.

We take notice that if Jesus did not come to earth, fulfill the Old Testament Scriptures, die for the sin of the world, and ascend back to His Father in heaven, we would have no hope. Our Christian hope is found only in Christ Jesus. He suffered so many things at the hands of humans to grant us the hope of eternal life. This type of hope cannot be produced by any human being because it is not a natural hope. We have an eternal hope that will carry us into eternity.

What is the meaning of hope? Hope is: to look forward to with confidence or expectation (the American Heritage College Dictionary).

Before coming to Christ, we were under the rule of Satan. Sin had the dominant rule over us, and we were without hope for a promising future. Then Jesus the Son of God, did the most wonderful thing for mankind. He gave His life to pay the eternal penalty for the sin of the world. Because of His loving, gracious, and merciful sacrifice, you, and I have Hope for eternal life. Make no mistake, you and I could never obtain the hope that Jesus has given to us. It is totally a gracious and merciful act of God. We could not approach God because of who He is, but through the atoning death of Jesus Christ we can come boldly to the throne of grace and receive hope in Him **(Romans 5:11 - And not only so, but we also joy in God through our Lord Jesus Christ, by whom we have**

now received the atonement).

Not only did Jesus give His life for us, but He also sent us His Holy Spirit to live inside of you and I, to empower us with the strength we need to please Him. The Spirit of Hope resides in the believer's heart for the rest of his/her life. This is a faith transaction and cannot be received by any other means. The Holy Spirit is the down payment and seal on your eternal life in Christ Jesus. We now have the promise of eternal life.

1) - This type of hope is enough to give every Christian Joy unspeakable and full of glory (1 Peter 1:8 - Whom having not seen, ye love; in whom, though now ye see Him not, yet believing, ye rejoice with joy unspeakable and full of glory). If you did not have hope in Christ, you would only have happiness which is conditional. It changes when ever your circumstances change. But to know that in this life, being filled with the Holy Spirit, you can have joy for the rest of your life. When life shifts and deal you an unpredictable hand, do not get upset just rest in Christ and His spiritual joy, because joy is what He gives. God is always there with and for you.

2) - God gives us joy in times of sufferings and testing (1 Peter 4:13 - But rejoice, inasmuch as ye are partakers of Christ's sufferings; that, when His glory shall be revealed, ye may be glad also with exceeding joy). Every believer in Christ knows that there will be days of testing and trials. We should also learn how to endure and keep our joy through these times. We are not to handle our problems as if there is no hope. We have the powerful person of the Holy Spirit living in the inside of us, supplying us with all the strength and joy we need to make it through one day at a time. Do not try to overrule the Holy Spirit, but give ear to hear the directions He will supply for your deliverance. Let Him lead and you follow.

***Remember to spend this week thanking God for all that He has done for you during your walk with Him as a Christian. As you think about all the things He has done, your joy should start maturing more and more.

Remember, the more you praise and thank God, the more joy you will experience.

Days 21 - 25
Trusting in God Brings Joy
Scripture Text
Psalm 33:20-21

20)-Our soul waiteth for the Lord: He is our help and shield. 21)-For our heart shall rejoice in Him, because we have trusted in His holy name.

This is a Psalm of praise to God for His goodness to His people. The children of God learned how to trust God from their heart, and it brought praise to Him and joy in them. They began to realize that they could not protect themselves from their enemies, so they had to trust God to do for them what they could not do for themselves.

The people of God knew if they called upon Him, He would hear them and come to care for them. They did not have to worry about anything as long as they placed their trust in God. There is a special bond that is formed between God and His people when they put their trust in Him. Not in some things but in all things. The heart rejoices when you trust in the name of the Lord. This is called the joy of the Lord.

We must learn how to wait on the Lord to do the things He desire to do in our lives. Waiting on Him will bring joy to your soul. Trusting God comes from believing that what He said He will do in His Word, He will do. This is where your faith must be active. It takes faith to trust God. Once you start trusting Him you will have joy. **This is the formula - Faith in God + Trust in God =Joy in You!**

As you mature in Christ, your level of trust in Him must also mature. Once you start casting your cares in the hands of God, you will have less worry and more rejoicing **(1 Peter 5:7 - Casting all your care upon Him, for He careth for you).** It is God's desire and great pleasure to be faithful to his servants by fulfilling His promises in their lives.

Learning how to place your cares, everyday living, and troubles upon God will take studying the Word of God (Bible) daily. As you read and learn the promises of God for yourself, you must trust that God will keep His promises to you. The only way to know that God will come through for you is to wait for Him to move. Can you do this?

1) - Being a Christian places you in right standing with God, this should give you rejoicing and gladness of heart (Psalm 64:10 - The righteous shall be glad in the Lord and shall trust in Him; And the upright in heart shall glory). Because you accepted Jesus to be your redeemer, you are now the righteousness of God through Christ Jesus. God credits you with the righteousness of His Son because you believe in Him. Now the Spirit of joy lives in you. Have faith and trust in His word, to keep nutrients flowing to your joy, so that it will mature.

2) - Trusting in God to be your help and strength will bring rejoicing and praise to your heart (Psalm 28:7 - The Lord is my strength and my shield; my heart trusted in him, and I am helped: therefore, my heart greatly rejoiceth; and with my song will I praise him). The more trust you put in God, the more things you become aware of that God is already doing in your life. You will find Him as your shield of protection, help in time of trouble, and joy in sadness. You will see that He is there all the time caring for you. This is awareness of the love and care of your God for you!

3) - Now that you are trusting God for your care, directing your path, and keeping you on the right course, you will have the fullness of joy (Psalm 16:11 - Thou will shew me the path of life: in thy presence is the fullness of joy; at thy right hand there are pleasures for evermore). This will allow you to experience such great joy, because you trust in the Almighty God to have His way in your life. Your joy is sure to mature, and you are sure to produce fruit for Him.

***This week should be an awesome week for you because your trust level grew along with your spiritual fruit of joy. The reason this is so important in the Christian's life, is because others will see the maturity of your joy and will desire to follow you as you follow Christ.

You must remember (Matthew 5:14 - Ye are the light of the world. A city that is set on a hill cannot be hid). So, mature your joy and let your light shine!

Days 26 - 30

Live Your Life in the Strength of Joy

Scripture Text

Psalm 97:11-12

11)-Light is sown for the righteous, and gladness for the upright in heart. 12)-Rejoice in the Lord, ye righteous; and give thanks at the remembrance of His holiness.

The Christians will never have to walk in sadness or shame because the light is sown for them. Meaning that God will remember whatever harvest you have sown. It may appear to you that God has forgotten, but please rest assured that God will never forget what you have done. You may have trial and tribulations, but your harvest will surely come forth in God's timing. So, live your life in the strength of the joy of the Lord every day. Do not waste time complaining about what it looks like. Sing praises to God for what He is doing for you behind the scenes.

You may even sow in tears, but you shall reap in joy **(Psalm 126:5-6 - 5)-They that sow in tears shall reap in joy. 6)-He that goeth forth and weepeth, bearing precious seed, shall doubtless come again with rejoicing, bringing his sheaves with him).** When you trust in God from your heart in sincerity, you will not lose any of your harvest.

God is Holy, perfect, and divine in nature. Whatever He promises in His Word, He will do. There is never a reason to doubt or question His ability to produce whatever He promised. We learned to trust God last week, now we put in action that trust to wait on His timing for the promise. As you remember all that He has already done for you, confidence and assurance should carry you through whatever you may be facing.

While you wait, get into the habit of rejoicing, giving thanks, and praising Him for Who He is. Let the Lord know that you are willing to wait on Him because you trust Him. You belong to God, and whatever path He has chosen for you will always be the best path. Take confidence in knowing that you can walk in joy as you grow in God's grace. Joy will give you the strength you need to make it to the finish line.

1) Committing your ways unto the Lord will bring you joy because you will allow Him to direct your path (Proverbs 3:5-6 - 5)-Trust in the Lord with all thine heart; and lean not unto thine own understanding. 6)-In all thy ways acknowledge Him, and He shall direct thy paths). True joy also comes from following the leading and guidance of the Holy Spirit. As you acknowledge Him in all of your ways, the joy of the Lord will be your strength. Start surrendering your ways unto Him and watch how joyful you become. It is sure to happen.

2) - Giving thanks to God is another contributor to living in joy (Psalms 136:1 - O give thanks unto the Lord, for He is good: for His mercy endureth forever). Giving thanks to God shows your respect for His goodness and mercy towards you and also for who He is. Thanksgiving should be what you give to God at all times. When we learn to be thankful, we find less time to complain. Complaining is one sure way to stunt the maturity of your joy. It places you in a spirit of entitlement and have you thinking that God owes you something all the time. Being thankful allows you to see that everything you have was given to you by God, and He did not have to do it, but by grace He did it anyway.

Start getting up in the morning praising and thanking God in everything, and watch Him bring you to a place you never thought you would be.

3) - Get serious in studying the word of God and making this a daily part of your life (2 Timothy 2:15 - Study to shew thyself approved unto God, a workman that needeth not to be ashamed, rightly dividing the word of truth). You owe it to yourself to become wise in the things of God. The more you know about God the closer you walk with Him. The closer you are to Him, the more joyful you become because your trust level in Him grows. From the beginning of creation until now, God has always pursued a relationship with His people. Draw closer to Him and give Him the opportunity to draw closer to you. Let it be a mutual relationship.

4) - Walking in Christ Jesus from day to day requires joy. As we remember the things God has spoken unto us in His word, we will have joy and it will remain in us (John 15:11 - These things have I spoken unto you, that, my joy might remain in you, and that your joy might be full). Pray and walk in the Holy Spirit to mature your spiritual fruit of joy.

*****This is the final week to work on maturing your spiritual fruit of joy.**
Remember, practice makes perfect. Give it all you have to walk in the joy of the Lord daily!

NOTES

Month Six - Maturing the Fruit of Peace

Days 1 - 5

Serving God in Peace

Scripture Text

John 14:27

Peace I leave with you, my peace I give unto you: not as the world giveth, give I unto you. Let not your heart be troubled, neither let it be afraid.

In this Scripture Jesus is getting ready to leave His disciples and return back to heaven to be with His Father. He is giving them His assurance of better days for them and the world. His disciples did not understand what was being taught to them at that time, but they always knew that Jesus had a purpose behind whatever He taught them. They just needed to hear Him, and Jesus would bring it to pass. Later they would understand just what He was teaching them.

As long as Jesus was on the earth walking with them, everything was great. But now that He is completing the mission He was sent to do, He knew they would suffer discouragement, disarray, and complete disappointment for a while. Notice, it was for a little while because Jesus knew that He was going away to send back all the help they would ever need, to complete their assignments.

1) - This help would be in the person of the Holy Spirit (John 14:16 - And I will pray the Father, and He shall give you another comforter, that he may abide with you forever). He would be sent to live or abide in them, to give them the comfort that Jesus had given them in person. This is so very awesome to know how much Jesus cared for them, and now for us. Jesus knew they would need peace to continue serving Him as required. Nothing else would replace the need for God's peace.

Peace means freedom from quarrels and disagreement; Harmonious

relations; Inner contentment; Serenity (the American Heritage College Dictionary).

Jesus promised them that He would leave His peace with them, and He would also give His peace to them. It would not be like the peace of the world which may be here today but gone tomorrow. The peace Jesus is promising to them would be an everlasting peace, because it would be included in the fruit of the Holy Spirit. Once the Christian receives the Spirit of Christ, he is empowered with the peace of God. Because God is eternal, His peace is also eternal, meaning everlasting. Yes, you can have this peace forever. This is a deep tranquility of your mind, a peace that keeps you calm in the midst of bad situations and circumstances. This peace is not governed by conditions and environments because it is secure in the Holy Spirit. The peace of God works from the inside outward. Therefore, it cannot be controlled by other because it abides in you. This makes you responsible for allowing the Holy Spirit to mature your peace as you follow Him.

2) - It is hard to do anything when you are always troubled, discouraged, and fearful. This is why Jesus promised to send back help to fix all of these major problems. Peace is also a fruit of the Spirit. It is given to the believer to unify with God and one another (Galatians 5:22a - But the fruit o the Spirit is love, joy, peace). When the body of Christ cannot walk in peace, it is almost impossible to serve God. It is hard to love and trust one another without peace. The lack of peace will limit the move of God in your life on every level. Please work on maturing your fruit of peace so that you can serve God in the full capacity of His will for your life.

Peace plays an important role in your love and service for God. Walking in peace also contribute to keeping your joy full. How can you have joy without peace? How can you serve God in confidence without peace?

3) - It is the will of God that you have this peace that He spoke of in His word. Jesus knew that you would have tribulations and problems,

but He overcame the world so that you would be able to abide in His peace (John 16:33 - These things I have spoken unto you, that in me ye might have peace. In the world ye shall have tribulation: but be of good cheer; I have overcome the world). These are just a few things to consider about your relationship without the peace of God. Serving God is the greatest assignment you will ever have. Do not hinder your walk with Him because you do not mature your spiritual fruit of peace.

***Why live in confusion and disarray when you can live a full life in the peace of God? This week make the ultimate choice to do all that is within you to mature your peace fruit.

Remember, serve God with gladness from a heart of tranquility and assurance.

Days 6 - 10

Your Faith Have Saved You, Go in Peace

Scripture Text

Luke 7:50

And He said to the woman, thy faith hath saved thee; go in peace.

This was a teaching moment for Jesus at the home of Simon. Jesus was invited to the home of Simon to eat with Simon and some of his guests. While they were there, a woman who was a sinner, came into the house bringing an alabaster box of ointment and crying. She begin to wash Jesus' feet with her tears, drying His feet with her hair, kissing His feet, and anointing His feet with the ointment she brought in with her. Many who were present judged her and felt that Jesus should turn her away because of who and what she was.

Jesus took the opportunity to teach them all a very valuable lesson on forgiveness. He gave a parable regarding the fact that since He entered the house, no one offered Him any water to wash His feet or anything else. But this woman did all of this for Him. After teaching, Jesus summed the matter up by telling all who were present, that the woman's sins are many and she is forgiven for much, for she loved much. But to whom little is forgiven, the same loveth little. So, Jesus turns to the woman and tells her, your faith have saved you, go in peace.

This somehow reminds me of us all. We were sinners, but God forgave us of all our sins and told us to go in peace. He let us know in the holy Scriptures, that it is by faith we are saved and not of any work on our part. He also made a point to inform us that if we were forgiven of much sin, we would love Him with much love. But when you feel like you were not forgiven of much sin, you will not love much. My question to you is, do you love a little or do you love a lot?

1) - This is so awesome because if you do not understand the depth of how much you were forgiven, you will not understand why the peace of God is so important for your survivor as a Christian. For we all have sinned and come short of God's glory (Romans 3:23 - For all have sinned and come short of the glory of God). We should never look on anyone as being worst than others because we were all sinners at one point in our lives.

This woman was not too pride to fall down at the feet of Jesus in the presence of others, who looked upon her as nothing and nobody. She knew who she was and what she was guilty of doing. She also knew about Jesus and how he could cleanse her of all the problems she had. She humbled herself to receive the forgiveness and peace of God she so desperately needed. She came into Jesus' presence crying and upset but when she left, she went out in the peace of God!

Jesus died for the sin of the world from His heart. He was motivated by love to submit to such treatment from humans for our benefit. When I think of all that Jesus suffered for our eternal salvation, it humbles my heart to desire to give Him everything that He desires of me. This should be our top priority in life.

Once the Holy Spirit comes into the Christian's heart, He brings with Him the deposit of peace as one of the traits of the Spirit. This is why it is known as one of the fruit of the Spirit. Every Christian is given this type of peace from God to keep him/her united together with God and one another.

2) - We are to walk in unity, but it cannot happen if we do not possess the peace of God in our hearts (Colossians 3:15 - And let the peace of God rule in your hearts, to the which also ye are called in one body: and be ye thankful). It is very important that you allow the Holy spirit to rest, rule, and abide in your heart, to lead and guide you into the place where your spiritual fruit of peace will prosper and mature. Because you do not know what it will take for your fruit to mature, obey the Holy Spirit in all areas of your life, so that He can aid you into proper fruit maturity. It is up to you as to how much peace you have in your life.

Take full advantage of the spiritual help the Holy Spirit is willing to give you. **Keep in remembrance, that your faith in God saved you, now you can go in the Peace of God!**

***If you are experiencing confusion, disarray, unrest, or anything else that is causing you disruption of God's peace in your life, please spend this entire week looking into your heart to locate the source of the problem.

Remember, seek the guidance of the Holy Spirit to show you what is wrong and work on regaining your peace.

Days 11 - 15

Keep Your Mind on Jesus and Walk in Peace

Scripture Text

Isaiah 26:3

Thou wilt keep him in perfect peace, whose mind is stayed on thee: because he trusteth in thee.

From a song of rejoicing, we are told that our God will keep us in perfect peace if we keep our minds stayed on Jesus, because we trust Him. **God is saying that He will (a promise) keep us in PERFECT peace if (conditional) we keep our minds stayed on Him.** We have an obligation to keep our minds on Jesus if we want to experience this perfect peace in God's promise. Many people want this peace but do not know what to do to keep their mind stayed on Jesus. How do you keep your mind stayed on Jesus daily?

1) - To keep your mind stayed on Jesus, you must think on things that are honest, true, just, and pure. These are just a few things that should be kept on your mind (Philippians 4:8-9 - 8)-Finally, brethren, whatsoever things are true, whatsoever things are honest, whatsoever things are just, whatsoever things are pure, whatsoever things are lovely, whatsoever things are of good report; if there be any virtue, and if there be any praise, think on these things. 9)-Those things, which ye have both learned, and received, and heard, and seen in me, do: and the God of peace shall be with you). To get different results, you must commit to doing different things. These are requirements listed in the Scriptures.

When you walk in the peace of God, you will show God and others how much you really trust God with your life. It is one thing to say you trust God, but the evidence is when others can see it by the way you walk before

God. Obey the Scriptures and you will keep the peace of God flowing in your heart.

Peace should be what you do daily. It is never enough to tell others how much you trust God, people want to see it in the way you carry yourself on a daily basis. God already knew that we all would have problem in this world, so He made provisions for each of us through His redemptive plan of salvation. Jesus included in His Holy Spirit the fruit of peace so that there would be a difference in the way we handled our affairs, versus the way the world shows their peace.

2) - Jesus said His peace He gives to you, and it is not like the world (John 14:27a - Peace I leave with you, my peace I give unto you: not as the world giveth, give I unto you). Because this peace is given by God it is guaranteed to produce in you the lifestyle that God promised it would, if you adhere to the instructions given in the Scriptures.

The formula in Scripture says to think on things that are honest. As your think on things that are honest your heart will feed on honesty. As you think on things that are just, it feeds your heart justice. The same is true with things that are pure, lovely, and of good report. You will get out what you put in. So, avoid things that are sure to break your peace, like gossip, complaining, putting down others, thinking evil of others, and being a talebearer. This type of behavior should not be a part of your Christian walk any way. So as your fruit mature, start weeding out these behaviors.

Take the time this week to work on avoiding things that will disrupt your constant peace. This alone will help your fruit to mature. Do not get pulled into conversations that you know will break your peace. Sometimes you can speak on things that will cause you to become uneasy about someone else. Avoid these potholes and hold tight to your peace.

***This week, it is important to be spiritually minded, avoiding all of these things **(Romans 8:6 - For to be carnally minded (fleshly) is death; but to be spiritually minded is life and peace).** You must walk by the directing of the Holy Spirit at all times.

Remember, prayer is much needed to get these things out of your life. Pray, Pray, and Pray!

Days 16 - 20
Listen to the Voice of God
Scripture Text
Psalm 85:8

I will hear what God the Lord will speak: for He will speak peace unto His people, and to His saints: but let them not turn again to folly.

This Scripture was written during a time when the people of God was suffering from distress after their disobeying the commandments of God. They were in a dry place in life and needed God to come and bless them again. The people knew that since God had blessed them before, He was able to do it again, if they would return unto him. True repentance from their heart was needed, not just lip service.

Once they realized that they were in this predicament because of their own actions, they knew only God could fix the problem. God really loved them, and did not want His people to suffer, but their sins had brought them to this place. Their attention was now directed back to the will of God, and they wanted to hear what God would say to them. They knew time after time God had forgiven their sins and brought them back into His good grace. This time was no difference from before.

The people of God knew that when they returned back to God that He would speak peace to them. They all understood what it was like to live in the peace that God provided for them, and they craved for this peace once again. They also knew they could not return back to the folly (disregard to the will or things of God) that got them in this situation. Now they wanted to hear from Him, **"Speak Lord for Your Servants Listens".**

When God fills us with His Holy Spirit, it is so peaceful to walk with Him. This is a peace that you have never experienced before, and you know that you want to experience this forever. But sometimes as life happens you may experience a shift in your peaceful status. You may find yourself easy to be distracted, grumpy with others more than not, and just not feeling like yourself, because your peace is disrupted.

1) - When your peace is disrupted, this is a sure sign that you need to invest spending secret time with the Lord. Put your mind on Him and communicate with Him in prayer, and you need to do it right away. The longer you stay this way, the more you will worry and fret over your issues (Isaiah 26:3-Thou will keep him in perfect peace, whose mind is stayed on thee: because he trusteth in thee). You have to constantly put all of your trust in God to keep maturing your peace fruit. You will find rest in the Lord as you trust in Him.

2) - Your peace is so important in your relationship with God and others because it promotes unity. Not only this but Jesus said for you to follow peace with all men (Hebrews 12:14 - Follow peace with all men, and holiness, without which no man shall see the Lord). You must pursue peace from your heart and the same peace will live in your heart. This fruit is to mature to keep you in the peaceful life God meant for you to have. How long are you willing to go without experiencing the peace of God on the mature level? Do not waste any more time, seek peace.

3) - Listening to the voice of God will enable you to live the peace of God which passes all understanding (Philippians 4:7 - And the peace of God, which passeth all understanding, shall keep your hearts and minds through Christ Jesus). When you can obey the voice of God and find joy in doing so, you will have the peace of God operating in your life daily. Your peace will mature with you because you are doing the will of God. The peace of God comes from listening and obeying the voice of God. Please have a sensitive ear to hear when the Spirit of God Speaks to you.

***This week stay in the Word of God daily and make sure you are attentive to hearing His voice. After hearing Him, please heed everything God is telling you to do. Do not talk yourself out of obeying His voice, because the more you override His voice the easier it becomes. This is a sure way to start being disobedient to God.

Remember, this week walk daily in the peace of God totally. The easier it is to disobey God's voice the less mature your spiritual fruit of peace becomes.

Days 21 - 25

Confidence In God's Peace

Scripture Text

Romans 5:1

Therefore, being justified by faith, we have peace with God through our Lord Jesus Christ.

This Scripture is letting us know, that peace is one of the results that Christians have because we are justified (declared righteous) by faith in Jesus Christ. This peace is not just any peace, it is the peace of God that is given to the believers because of the new relationship with God through His Son, Jesus.

God recognizes that we accept His testimony about Jesus and all that God said about His son, now it is accredited to us as the righteousness of God. We are no longer enemies of God, but spiritually adopted sons of the Most High God. Now we have the assurance and confidence in knowing that we are redeemed and no longer without hope of eternal life. We are now the temple of God, and must know without doubt that He will take care of us.

1) -We know we have a new life and the assurance that no matter what happens in our lives, we are the children of God (Romans 8:28 - And we know that all things work together for good to them that love God, to them who are the called according to His purpose). This alone gives you the confidence that you can live in the peace of God all the time. It is your choice of course. So, whatever happens in your life, God will work it out for your good.

2) - God gives you His peace, but you are responsible for keeping and maturing this fruit as you mature in Christ. You are not to remain babes in Christ, but to become mature so that you can produce fruit in Him (1Peter 2:2 - As newborn babes, desire the sincere milk of

the word, that ye may grow thereby). We are instructed by the Word of God to desire to grow in Christ. What is your desire? Do you want to grow and mature? You should never become satisfied in remaining a babe in Christ.

The more you grow in Christ the more confident you have in Him. You begin to blossom in your peace, and it will display through the way you live. You will seek the wisdom of God in everything you do, and the peace of God will lift you up above worrying and the cares of this life. You will avoid getting caught up in these things.

3) - You may not think this is possible, but you can truly have this type of peaceful confidence. It depends on how much and how close you decide to walk and invest in your relationship with God (Ephesians 3:12 - In whom we have boldness and access with confidence by the faith of Him). Keep your peace and walk in the confidence that only God can give. God does not expect you to make all of this happen on your own. He sent His Holy spirit to help you through the process. The Holy Spirit is your guide to maturity, always rely on Him.

4) - As you walk in the righteousness of God, His peace and assurance will remain with you forever (Isaiah 32:17 - And the work of righteousness shall be peace; and the effect of righteousness quietness and assurance forever). Maturing to the things of God will take time, so do not lose your peace while you journey through this adventure. Walking in the peace of God is not hard when you make it an adventure, and learn new things about God as you move forward. We are to learn of Him, and the best way to do this is to walk with Him on a daily basis. There should be constant excitement regarding your Spiritual walk in Christ.

***Take this week to study the Scriptures that are given and find the boldness and confidence the Holy Spirit is waiting to give you.

Remember, this is not something you can complete on your own, but the Spirit of God is here to help you live it out, one day at a time!

Days 26 - 30

Staying Spiritually Minded

Scripture Text

Romans 8:5-6

**5)-For they that are after the flesh do mind the things of the flesh;
but they that are after the Spirit the things of the Spirit. 6)-For to
be carnally minded is death; but to be spiritually minded is life
and peace.**

In these Scriptures the Lord is giving us direct teaching on the difference between being carnally minded (governed by your fleshly desires) and being spiritually minded (governed by the Holy Spirit). These two are always at war between each other, and at the end of the day one has won over the other. Which of the two are winning your time, energy, and efforts? Evaluate yourself and be honest in the process.

Your fleshly mind is the mind you were born with when you entered into the world. It is totally the mind you inherited from your earthly parents. This is the mind that always want attention, fleshly desires, and lust after the things that are contrary to the will of God. This is the mind that love having his way and will do whatever is necessary to make it happen. This mind is bad to the health of your spiritual growth and maturity. If you are led by this mind, you will eventually become what it is feeding you, selfishness!

This mind is always concerned with the physical and material thing of life and not very concerned with eternal issues. It is the mind that is not focused upon putting God first in whatever you do. This mind will make you happy for a while but later in life you will begin to want more spiritual substances that your flesh cannot provide.

1) - The carnal mind is not able to allow God to order your steps,

neither is it able to follow after the righteousness of God. Why? Because it needs to be transformed and renewed by the Spirit of God (Romans 12:2a - And be not conformed to this world: but be ye transformed by the renewing of your mind). A true transformation must happen for you to become spiritually minded.

The Spiritual mind is a mind of life and peace. This mind is renewed by the Spirit of God. It is no longer the mind you inherited from your parents. This mind is given to you by God when you are born again and filled with the Spirit of God. The reason it is a renewed mind is because you get a new mind at your new birth. This is called a fresh start (born again).

Now your mind is a mind of peace and is controlled by the Spirit of God. Just as Jesus walked in peace everywhere He went, so are you now to abide by the mind of Christ, and walk in this same peace. Your peace should be with you every day because you are walking in the Spirit and not in the flesh.

You are now concerned with the things that promote peace and abundant life. You are totally changed and given a new life, you are a new creature and old things are passed away. There are certain things you must start adjusting to with this new mind.

2) - With this new mind, your character must change to be in unity with your mind (Philippians 2:5 - Let this mind be in you, which was also in Christ Jesus). Christians are to have the same attitude and humility Jesus had, with genuine love for one another. Peace is promoted by love and unity inside of you and radiates outwards to others. Your peace is never separated from who you are, that is why you have a spiritual mind. Remember peace is a fruit of the Spirit living in you.

3) - Jesus took His peace with Him because it was a part of Him, and He instructed His disciples to do the same as they carried out His ministry (Matthew 10:12-13 - [12)]-And when you come into a house salute it. [13)]-And if the house be worthy, let your peace come upon it:

but if it be not worthy, let your peace return to you). Peace should be what you do because the Spirit of peace is in you.

It is very important to stay spiritually minded, because it allows you to walk in the Spirit of God. When you walk in the Spirit of God, obeying His word, following His directions, humbling yourself to his desires for your life, and following peace with all men, you will experience spiritual maturity of your fruit of peace.

4) - When you walk spiritually minded, you will not be a busy body or talebearer in other peoples' matters (Proverbs 26:20 - Where no wood is, there the fire goes out: so, where there is no talebearer, the strife cease). Being a busy body or a talebearer is sure to cause a disruption in your peaceful flow. Christians are to be mindful not to cause problems for others, due to being out of the will of God. It is the will of God that you mind you own business and care for the things that God has assigned to your hands. This alone will show how mature you are in your peaceful fruit production.

***Take this week to evaluate yourself in the fruit of peace and see if there is more that you can do to allow the Holy Spirit to mature your fruit of peace.

A few years ago, the Lord gave me a poem on peace, and I was shocked to see how often peace was spoken of in the Scriptures. I would like to share this poem with you to show you how important it is to have the mature peace of God in your life.

The Peace of God He Gives to ME

When Jesus was born in Bethlehem

No one knew He was the Great I Am

There was no room for Him that night

But the angels of God gave the shepherds a fright
Jesus came to bring this earth His peace
And set this world from Satan free
Isaiah spoke of Jesus in chapter fifty three
That He would be chastised for our peace
Paul said in Romans chapter five verse one
Justified by faith, have peace if you want
Philippians chapter four and verse seven
Gives peace for mind and heart to prepare for heaven
Galatians chapter five and verse twenty two
Offers peace as a fruit just to give to you
It is stated in Colossians that through Jesus blood on the cross
Peace was made plentiful for all that was lost
Second Timothy two and twenty two
Said flee from all sins, my peace I give to you
Second Corinthians thirteen in Paul's farewell
He recommends peace so you and I shall
Haggai the prophet in chapter two verse nine
Shows that God will give peace all the time
The peace of God He gives to me
I need and want it because it sets me free
When trials and turmoil come to hinder me
My mind I give to God for His peace

I never know what tomorrow may hold

Maybe good maybe bad, so much I'm told

But in my heart, I know I'm free

Because of the peace my God gives to me

Written by Dr. Catherine Braswell on11/19/2014 @ 11:00 am

Remember, please allow your fruit to mature so that you will have the peace of God that passes all understanding.

NOTES

Month Seven - Maturing the Fruit of Longsuffering

Days 1 - 5

Serving and Pleasing God While Walking in Longsuffering (Patience)

Scripture Text

Colossians 1:10-11

10)-That ye might walk worthy of the Lord unto all pleasing, being fruitful in every good work, and increasing in the knowledge of God: 11)-Strengthened with all might, according to His glorious power, and unto all patience and longsuffering with joyfulness.

When reading these Scriptures, many Christians do not see the power of God in the instructions for longsuffering. As you learn about longsuffering and patience, you may feel that there is not much to be desired. Besides, who want to wait or suffer for anything anymore? There are many lessons to be taught here if you are willing to learn them. To understand the importance of longsuffering, you must know exactly what it means, where it comes from, and why you need it.

Longsuffering means: Patiently enduring wrongs or difficulties; Patient (longsuffering, forbearance, bearing and enduring pain) endurance, perseverance, being constant, and steadfast. (the American Heritage College Dictionary).

Longsuffering is a trait of God, given to the believer in the person of the Holy Spirit, as a fruit of the Spirit. It is needed by the Christian to learn how to walk worthy of the Lord unto all pleasing. To be fruitful in every good work, and to increase in the knowledge of God. I have often heard in my walk as a Christian, it takes time to live holy. Over time I can truly say without doubt, this is true. It really takes time to live holy and to learn how to please God by faith. To get to true holy living, longsuffering is needed.

Do not think you will become a mature Christian over night. You must learn to study the word of God to increase in the knowledge of God. The more you learn and know about God, the closer you draw to Him and the more He draws to you. This will strengthen you with all might by the power of God. You will understand that it is not by your power that things happen in your life, but by the power of the Almighty God. He is the only one who can give you all the patience and longsuffering that you need to complete your walk as a Christian.

When God produce in you, patience, and longsuffering there is a deep joyfulness that floods your soul because you never thought you could experience such levels of this fruit called longsuffering.

1) - Serving God requires walking daily in longsuffering. It takes patience to allow God to move the way He desires in your life (Colossians 3:12-13a - 12)-Put on therefore, as the elect of God, holy and beloved, bowels of mercies, kindness, humbleness of mind, meekness, longsuffering: 13a)-Forbearing one another, and forgiving one another). You must learn how to be patient with others for as long as required by God. To do this you must realize that everyone is different, and they may not act or feel like you do as a Christian. Please understand that everyone does not mature at the same speed or rate, so you must wait patiently on them to grow, and forgive them when needed. This must be done in the spirit of love. Do not judge but love and understand where they are.

2) - Remember just because you see it your way, does not mean that your way is right (Proverbs 14:12 - There is a way which seemeth right unto a man, but the end thereof are the ways of death). Sometimes you may fail in the area of patience and longsuffering because you see and perceive things differently from others. Who is to say that you are always right? Longsuffering and patience will help you learn to listen to others also. Studying the truth of God's word will help you to understand that Jesus is the only real truth and if you are not lead by the Holy Spirit, your truth is simply your truth. This will also help to mature your fruit of longsuffering. So, in times of disagreements, you must be battled tested to develop mature fruit. Longsuffering will help you to stay the course in integrity, because you trust God. It will also enhance your love for you brothers and sisters.

3) - To serve and please God, you must be able to walk in the spiritual fruit of longsuffering. There will be times when you will need patience to wait on God to move in your life (Luke 8:15 - But that on the good ground are they, which in an honest and good heart, having heard the word, keep it, and bring forth fruit with patience). The longsuffering and patience of God will help you to bring forth fruit because you walk in the fruit of the Spirit. To please God, you must be able to allow God to move in His time and in His way. Without patience and longsuffering, you will find yourself doing things on your own and not waiting on Him. Please do not make this mistake because it can cause you a lot of trouble. Wait on God!

***This is the first week in longsuffering. Allow yourself to study on the fruit of longsuffering and find out why it is needed to serve God, and also how to please Him while you are serving. Work on your urge to take matters into your own hands, wait on God to show up in your situations.

Remember, it takes time to live holy and longsuffering (patience) will help you walk it out.

Days 6 - 10

Longsuffering (Patience) in Trials and Testing

Scripture Text

James 1:2-4

2)-My brethren, count it all joy when ye fall into divers temptations:
3)-Knowing this, that the trying of your faith worketh patience. 4)-
But let patience have her perfect work, that ye may be perfect and entire, wanting nothing.

We learn in this passage of Scripture, that the right attitude to have in times of trials and testing is joy. Joy and longsuffering works together during hard times, because the joy of the Lord is your strength. This strength is needed with longsuffering to help you not break under pressure. You may ask what pressures? Well, the truth is that every individual in this world will have trials and times of testing. By making wrong or poor choices, some trials and test, you may bring on yourself, while others will just drop in your life because you are human. Either way they are trials, and you will have to endure them. You cannot escape trials or testing but you can learn and grow from the experience with the right attitude.

As Christians, you are not to handle these times in your life as if you do not have hope. You are to rely on the Holy Spirit to lead you throughout these times. This is why it is so important to have mature spiritual fruit abiding in you. You must understand that as you are being tested, there are areas in your life that need to be changed, removed, or strengthened (the pruning process). This is done for your good and you will benefit from this. God is perfect and does not need to be tested, so the test is all about you and how you develop spiritually.

During this time in your life, it would help to remember that God knows the right test or trial to place in your life, and He knows the exact time to let it happen. I am not saying that it will be easy, but what I am saying is that you will not have to walk it alone. Knowing this, you will not have to worry about the why, but only concern yourself with the patience you need to endure, and the faith in God to trust that He will see you through.

Longsuffering must have her perfect work in your life, meaning that whatever the reason God allowed this to happen in your life was to make you better and not to discourage, punish, or defeat you. These trials will help to mature your spiritual fruit of longsuffering. Go through your time of testing and reap the rewards.

1) - Many times, when you are tested especially if it is often, defeat, despair, and discouragement starts to set in. You need to settle in and change your mind about how you are seeing your test. You are not just being tested, but you are also being tried and proven by the Almighty God (Job 23:10 - But He knoweth the way that I take: when He has tried me, I shall come forth as gold). Your trials will show you the purification power that the Holy Spirit possess in you. You will grow and develop more godly character as you stay the course. You will never know how much of you have been changed if you are never tested. Remember, gold must be tested by severe heat to prove the level of purity. So must you be tested to prove your level of purity unto God. Your heart must be pure before God.

2) - Do not allow negativity to be your first thought when the testing begin. Please think with a positive attitude knowing that the trials happened to produce patience in you (James 1:3 - Knowing this, that the trying of your faith worketh patience). When you trust God, you already know that nothing happens in your life without God knowing about it first. Since He knows about it, be sure He knows that you needed that trial in your life for an important purpose. This is when your endurance will show up in your life. You must be battled tested to fight and win the battle.

3) - Giving up is not an option. You must persevere and never give up. Never let your trials break you but let it make you strong (1Peter 2:20 - For what glory is it, if, when ye be buffeted for your fault, ye shall take it patiently? But if, when ye do well, and suffer for it, ye take it patiently, this is acceptable with God). Do not fret over the trial, allow God to get the glory out of your testing. You may ask why would God get glory out of your trials? The truth is, God knows the results you get will mold and make you into the vessel of His choice. Only God knows who and what you are meant to be in this life. Trust Him to complete His will.

***As you study this week, allow your mind to start changing regarding how you view your times of testing and trials. Make up in your mind that you are persuaded to follow Jesus, no matter what.

Remember, you stand to gain so much if you stay the course!

Days 11 - 15

You Must be Tested, Tried, and Proven

Scripture Text

Ephesians 4:1-2

1)-I therefore, the prisoner of the Lord, beseech you that ye walk worthy of the vocation wherewith ye are called, 2)-With all lowliness and meekness, with longsuffering, forbearing one another in love.

This Scripture is teaching us the need to walk worthy of being called a Christian. This new life demands that you walk as a child of light because you are no longer living in darkness. Whatever you were before Christ, is no longer welcomed in your new life in Christ Jesus. You are to walk humbly before God knowing that pride is never acceptable in this new relationship. Longsuffering and forbearing one another in love is required. You can have confidence but not pride.

To walk worthy of the call of God for your life requires that you be tested in all areas of life. Being tested is such an important need for your spiritual growth as a Christian. If you are never tested, how will you ever know what you can possibly endure. It is one thing to tell others what God can do for them, but what happens in your life when you are being tested in the same area? Once the test is started in your life, how do you respond? What type of attitude do you display? What do you really feel about God and how He allowed you to encounter this test?

There is a formula in the next part of this Scripture that is so powerful, because it instructs you in what things you must do to walk worthy of the vocation that you are called to do. **"With all lowliness and meekness, with longsuffering, forbearing one another in love".** This is the whole formula, meaning not prideful, having self-control, endurance, patience, and carry it out in love. You know it is so amazing to see the connection of each spiritual fruit and how they work together.

1) - You must always remember that your trials come to make you strong. God wants you to be a strong soldier for Him, able to endure whatever comes your way (Ephesians 6:10 - Finally, my brethren, be strong in the Lord, and in the power of His might). Please know that you are not left to yourself to produce this strength. It is in the power of God's might that you will stand the test. Knowing this one thing should encourage you to submit to God's testing. You will be tested many times in your life, having confidence in knowing that God will always be there for and with you to give you all the strength you need, should encourage you to stay the course. Embracing what God is doing will give you the greatest results.

2) - As gold is tried and proven to show the power and strength of the gold, you must be tested, tried, and proven to become more and more like Jesus (Job 23:10 - But He knoweth the way that I take: when He hath tried me, I shall come forth as gold). Last week we talked about being tested like gold for purity. You will be tried in areas that your trials are meant to produce strength and power in you. How will you know that you have grown if you are never tested in that thing? During the trying you will be able to praise God for bringing you through. You will see progress, strength, and power in your own life that you knew you did not have before the trial. You will be able to react differently now to situations, because your longsuffering and patience begin to mature, enabling you to walk more like Jesus. This is what your trials are meant to do.

***This is week three, you should take this week to pay attention to the areas that you see God testing you in, and ask Him to help you gain the results He want in your life. You are not living to please yourself, but to please the Almighty God!

Also remember, it is not by your power that you make it, but the power of God and your surrendering to his wisdom in testing you.

Days 16 - 20

You Must Keep Persevering

Scripture Text

Ephesians 6:13

Wherefore take unto you the whole armour of God, that ye may be able to withstand in the evil day, and having done all, to stand.

Longsuffering also means to persevere! To never give up, to stay with it no matter what. The apostle Paul wrote to The Ephesians Church telling them to take unto them the whole armour of God to be able to stand in the evil days. Paul is referring to the many trials that would come against the believers from the forces of evil. He knew that if the believer would stay fully clothed in their spiritual protective gears, they would be able to stand against anything that comes against them.

The believer is instructed to stand even when he/she has done all to stand. Paul's confidence is centered directly on the power of the whole armour of God. He had suffered so many things at the hands of many evil people, and he knew quite well the power that God's spiritual protective gears possess. He truly wanted them to understand how to stand. You must be spiritually dressed to succeed in life.

1) - He goes on to give a brief description of the armour He is speaking of to the believer. He tells them to:1)-have your loins girt about in truth (Jesus is the truth); 2)-have on the breastplate of righteousness (Jesus is our righteousness, cover your heart); 3)-your feet shod with the preparation of the gospel of peace (walk and run in peace); 4)-taking the shield of faith (walk by faith); 5)-the helmet of salvation (protect your mind for victory); 6)-the sword of the spirit, which is the word of God (stay in the word of God). When you walk fully dressed in your spiritual protective gears, you will mature and conquer, through perseverance. Spend valuable time in the word of God to keep your armour fitting properly, you must stay dressed to win! Keep on your spiritual outfit at all time.

2) - Paul knew that the Holy Spirit is equipped with everything you would ever need, to endure hardness as a good soldier. From experience, He had suffered so many hardships as he walked with the Lord by faith. He also look to Jesus as his example in sufferings and persevering, until the end (Hebrews 2:18 - For in that He himself suffered being tempted, He is able to succour them that are tempted). Jesus, because He suffered in the flesh, is more than able to assist you in time of want, difficulty, distress, and need throughout your relationship with Him. He never slumber or sleep, so he is always available to see you through.

3) - When trials and temptations confronts you , rest in the knowledge that your God is faithful and He will not allow you to be tested above what you can stand (1Corinthians 10:13 - There has no temptation taken you but such as is common to man: but God is faithful, who will not suffer you to be tempted above that ye are able; but will with the temptation also make a way to escape, that ye may be able to bear it). Your God is always faithful to His word. He will make a way for you to escape that situation before it can take you out. The problem is not God, but will you use the escape route that God made for you. This is where your perseverance in you stands tall and sure like a rock. Your ability to hear God speak to you is very important in times of testing and temptation. If the Lord gives you an escape route, do not be proud and allow yourself to fall into the trap trying to prove something to people. Just obey the leading of the Holy Spirit.

***This week spend much time listening to the voice of God as He speaks to you. **Pay close attention to what He tells you to do and please obey Him.** This is how you develop longsuffering, perseverance, and patience in obeying the voice of God.

Remember, your spiritual fruit of longsuffering must grow to maturity. Allow God to help you in this area.

Days 21 - 25

Longsuffering Produces Obedience to God

Scripture Text

Hebrews 5:8-9

8)-Though He (Jesus) were a Son yet learned He obedience by the things which He suffered. 9)-And being made perfect, He became the author of eternal salvation unto all them that obey Him.

This Scripture is teaching us the fact that Jesus, the Son of God, was sent into this world to suffer for the sin of all mankind. Yet being the Son of God, he had to suffer many things even while obeying the will of His Father. This Scripture says that even being a Son, He learned obedience by the things which He suffered. The sufferings that He endured made Him obedient to God the Father. Longsuffering produces obedience to God, and obedience is something that every Christian will need to have in their lives. You cannot live for Jesus if you cannot obey Him.

Jesus was tempted by Satan in the wilderness before starting His earthly ministry. He used the Holy Scriptures to resist the devil and prevailed in obedience to His Father. I know you may say He was God's Son, and this is true, but Jesus had never experienced this before in His human flesh. Not only did He resist Satan in the wilderness, but He also went to the cross to pay the debt for sin that He did not owe, for you and me. This was longsuffering at its highest peak, but Jesus endured without fail and pleased His Father in the process. Suffering was a vital part of His making and in pleasing His Heavenly Father.

He did not complain but submitted to God's will for His life. Because He obeyed God, after completing His "Divine Assignment", Jesus became the author of eternal salvation to all that obey Him. This means that eternal salvation is available to everyone who obeys Jesus Christ! To walk as a Christian, we must obey God.

1) - Just as Jesus learned obedience through the things He suffered, the same is true for you and I (1Peter 4:1a - Forasmuch then as Christ hath suffered for us in the flesh, arm yourselves likewise with the same mind). Obedience is necessary in the Christian walk, and it is produced by the things you suffer as you mature in longsuffering. You must have the same mind as Christ to endure temptation, trial, and testing. Jesus did not give up and you must not give up.

2) - As you purpose in your heart to obey God, know that it will happen as you change your mind to the mind of Christ. God is longsuffering and He withholds His judgment on mankind waiting for them to repent (1Timothy 1:16 - Howbeit for this cause I obtained mercy, that in me first Jesus Christ might shew forth all longsuffering, for a pattern to them which should hereafter believe on Him to life everlasting). You have been chosen of God to be an example of longsuffering to the world. This is a part of what you have been called to do. Longsuffering is given as a fruit of the Spirit, and the reason it is given is to provide you with all the help you need during times of testing. You are not alone in the process.

As you walk in obedience unto God and allow Him to mature your spiritual fruit of longsuffering, count it all joy, knowing that you will benefit as this fruit matures.

***This week walk in total obedience to God as you endure temptation, trial, testing, or whatever you may encounter. Also remember, that suffering is a part of life, and everyone will go through suffering at some point.

Remember, your experience can be productive when you allow God to be there with you, as you learn all about longsuffering.

Days 26 - 30

Longsuffering - The Spiritual Fruit

Scripture Text

Galatians 5:22

But the fruit of the spirit is love, joy, peace, longsuffering, gentleness, goodness, faith.

Longsuffering is a virtue (moral excellence and righteousness) of the Holy Spirit, given to every Christian by God through the indwelling of the Holy Spirit. In Scripture it is known as a fruit of the Spirit. There are nine mentioned in this passage of Scripture, but I would like to take this week to really expound on LONGSUFFERING! This is a part of God's nature and He placed it inside of the Holy Spirit as a fruit. When the Spirit of God lives in you, the fruit of longsuffering lives in your as well.

There is so much pain and suffering in the world today. Many people are asking and wondering what to do or where to turn. There seems to be no solutions in sight. In fact, it seems to get worst before better. People are blaming one another for the problems they are experiencing and even this does not seem to help. **Please remember, Satan is the accuser of the brethren (Revelation 12:10 - And I heard a loud voice saying in heaven, now is come salvation, and strength, and the kingdom of our God, and the power of His Christ: for the accuser of our brethren is cast down, which accused them before our God, day and night).**

Satan is your spiritual adversary and in your human body you are no match for him. This is exactly why you need Jesus Christ, to let His Holy spirit live inside of you. The Holy Spirit will give you everything you need to defeat this enemy.

Many ask why doesn't God fix this? We must all remember that God, in creation gave man free choice, and because of this, man is able to

choose between right and wrong (Joshua 24:15a - And if it seems evil unto you to serve the Lord, choose you this day whom you will serve). It is sad, but many times we choose wrong over right, and God has to allow us to have our choices. Just as He has given us the free will to choose right or wrong, He also has made a solution to our sin problems. You must make the choice to serve God.

We all know that we live in a sinful world, and because of this, evil at its highest level is destroying so much of what God made to be good and very good. **God sent Jesus into this world, to enable us to escape the bondage of sin. He knew we would never be able to repair the broken relationship between God and man, on our own. Jesus took the divine assignment, came to die on the cross for the sin of the world (John 1:29 - the next day John seeth Jesus coming unto him, and saith, behold the Lamb of God which taketh away the sin of the world).** He rose again with all power in His hands. Even in this He still gives man free choice.

Man is now able to choose to accept what Jesus did for all of mankind or reject His offer of eternal salvation. If you choose to accept Jesus as your personal Savior, then you will receive His Gift of the Holy Spirit, to live inside of you forever. You can say no to His eternal plan of salvation and face life on your own.

Sin will always be in the earth until Jesus return again, but the Christian can experience hope in longsuffering, while you wait through the spiritual fruit of longsuffering (Romans 5:3-4 - [3)]-And not only so, but we glory in tribulations also: knowing that tribulation worketh patience; [4)]-And patience, experience; and experience, hope).

While you may have trials and temptation, the Holy Spirit through the spiritual fruit of longsuffering will give you patience to wait on God for His deliverance. He will give you perseverance to never give in or break under pressure. The Holy Spirit will give you endurance to conquer the trial and you become the victor and not the victim

(1Corinthians 10:13 - There hath no temptation taken you but such as is common to man: but God is faithful, who will not suffer you to be tempted above that you are able; but will with the temptation also make a way to escape, that ye may be able to bear it). Accept Jesus' remedy for sin.

One of the reasons the fruit of the Spirit include longsuffering, is to help you to endure through, and pass every trial, test, and temptation that will come into your life. **This does not mean that you will not experience pain, hurt, disappointment, or discouragement, but you can come forth as a mature Christian walking in the power of God (Hebrews 2:18 - For in that He himself hath suffered being tempted, he is able to succor (assist) them that are tempted).** Remember that no one told you the road would be easy, but God will not bring you this far to leave you. Jesus promised to never leave or forsaken you.

Please spend this week learning and understanding why maturing your spiritual fruit of longsuffering is so important in your walk with Jesus Christ. Also make a point of enduring under pressure.

NOTES

Month Eight - Maturing the Fruit of Gentleness

Days 1 - 5

What is Gentleness (Kindness)

Scripture Text

1 Thessalonians 2:4-7

**4)-But as we were allowed of God to be put in trust with the gospel,
even so we speak; not as pleasing man, but God, which trieth the
hearts. 5)-For neither at any time used we flattering words, as ye
know, nor a cloak of covetousness; God is witness: 6)-Nor of men
sought we glory, neither of you, nor yet of others, when we might
have been burdensome, as the apostles of Christ. 7)-But we were
gentle among you, even as a nurse cherisheth her children.**

In these Scriptures, the Apostle Paul reminded the Thessalonica Church that when he first came to preach the Gospel to them, his motives were pure. He did not come wanting anything from them, just to preach the gospel of Jesus Christ. Paul knew that God had trusted him with the Gospel message and allowed him to speak the word of God boldly to them. Not to the pleasing of man but unto God.

He stated that even after being treated very shameful, harshly, and suffering many things at the hands of people, he still came with a humble spirit and not seeking any glory from them. In fact, Paul said he was gentle among them as a nurse cherisheth (to treat with affection and tenderness) her children. He was well aware of the fact that God looks, tries, and judges the heart of man.

Paul operated in the fruit of gentleness when and wherever he encountered the people of God. He understood that being filled with the Spirit of God empowered him to walk in the virtue of his Father. Meaning, Paul was sent out by God to represent Him in all things and at all times. There was never a moment in his walk with Christ, that Paul could walk and do as he please. He was to be a gentle vessel of God, doing the commands of his master.

What is gentleness and why is it so important in the Christian's life?

1) - Gentleness is - 1)-Being considerate or kind in disposition, amiable and tender. 2)-Not harsh or severe; mild and soft. 3)-Easily manage or handled.

This is kindness in operation from your heart. This type and level of kindness cannot be acquired by your natural doings. It has to come from a source greater than yourself. It comes from the Holy Spirit being present in your heart. This is why it is called a fruit of the Spirit. This fruit will enable you to be considerate of others, kind in character and demeanor. The Holy Spirit will tenderize your heart to make you mild and soft. You will become easy to manage and not always ready to fight and disagree with others. Can you imagine the Holy Spirit transforming you into such a peaceful and kind individual? Well, it can happen.

2) - Gentleness is so important in the Christian's life because you are to go into all the world and teach the Gospel of Jesus Christ (Matthew 28:19 - Go ye therefore, and teach all nations, baptizing them in the name of the Father, and of the Son, and of the Holy Ghost). Being under the commands of God to work with His people, you must be approachable and able to get along with others that are not like you. The only way to do this is to have the spiritual fruit of gentleness (kindness), in your heart operating at full capacity. God knew before He told you to go, that you would need all the help and power you could get from Him to make this happen. You are to trust and obey what He tells you to do in order to reap the proper benefits.

3) - You will never be alone while you are walking in Him and He in you (Matthew 28:20b - And lo, I am with you always, even unto the end of the world. Amen). God was reassuring all of us that the Spirit of God would come back to dwell inside of us just as Jesus promised. The Holy Spirit would be the divine power needed to carry out God's word in our lives. This is why we MUST OBEY His leading and mature in Him as we fulfill the assignments of God.

***This is week one of Gentleness! Take all this time to learn the importance of allowing the Holy Spirit to lead you in everything you are doing in your life. Practice following and not leading the Holy Spirit when He speaks to your heart.

Remember, the spiritual fruit of gentleness is controlled by the Holy Spirit and your obedience to Him will produce maturity of the fruit!

Days 6 - 10

Being Gentle and Kind to One Another

Scripture Text

2Timothy 2:24

And the servant of the Lord must not strive; but be gentle unto all men, apt to teach, patient.

The Lord is instructing all Christians to be gentle to everyone. There are no exceptions to this rule. Kindness is to be applied in every situation. We are not to pick and choose to whom we will show this gentleness. Just as God shows His kindness to you, you are to show the same kindness to others. Kindness is who God is and because His Spirit lives in you, this is who you are.

You may not walk like this, but believe me this is who you are. Gentleness is what others should be able to see in your life all the time. Sure, there will be days when you may not come completely up to the full measure of the fruit, but you should not be far from the mark. You should have an honest heart to show gentleness and kindness to everyone you encounter whether they are a Christian or not.

God expects His children to be imitators of Him at all times, because you never know what God's plan may be for the individual as you present God to them. You never know what the person is going through, and you may be that one last hope for them. Always be gentle so that you will leave something positive in their memory. You may be sent to teach or encourage someone, being gentle and kind may soften their hearts to be receptive to the message.

1) - Being gentle means, not speaking evil of others and arguing with people. Remember you were not gentle until you became a Christian (Titus 3:2-4 - [2)-]To speak evil of no man, to be no brawlers,

but gentle, shewing all meekness unto all men. [3]-For we ourselves also were sometimes foolish, disobedient, deceived, serving divers lusts and pleasures, living in malice and envy, hateful and hating one another. [4]-But after that the kindness and love of God our Saviour toward man appeared). When you walk in gentleness and treat people in kindness you are admitting to others that you were not always walking right. That you were foolishly walking after the cares of this world and obeying the lusts of your fleshly cravings, and you needed the grace, mercy, and kindness of God to come and rescue you from this bondage. Now that you have been delivered, but not of your own power, you know the stronghold Satan had over your life, now you must show the same kindness to others as they struggle too. Just knowing this should make you desire to be a very gentle person. Please be kind to others as Christ is kind to you.

2) - When you are totally aware of the fact, that without God you could be doing everything everyone else is doing. This should prompt you to depend more and more upon the Holy Spirit to mature your fruit of gentleness. Do not be judgmental of anyone (Galatians 6:1 - Brethren, if a man be overtaken in a fault, ye which are spiritual, restore such a one in the spirit of meekness; considering thyself, lest thou also be tempted). Christians should never be judgmental of anyone because you do not know what tomorrow may hold for you. Today it may be someone else, but tomorrow it could be you. You are called upon by God to show love and kindness to everyone and leave all the judging to the Almighty God. Man looks at the outward appearance, but God always looks at the heart of the individual. God knows the inside scoop, you do not have that information! Your responsibility is to show kindness to all people at all times.

3) - It should be the desire of every individual to be kind and show kindness to all mankind (Proverbs 19:22a - The desire of a man is his kindness). When God has changed your heart, it should be your desire to continue walking in the newness of that change. Work with the Holy Spirit to mature your fruit of gentleness, because it makes you show the image of God in your life. Gentleness is a powerful trademark for the Christian, and it is sure to please God. Treat others as you desire to be treated because kindness will take you a long way in life.

***This is week two on gentleness! Spend time being kind to others even if they are not kind to you, it is the will of God. Trusting God to lead you with His kindness will bring great results.

Remember, you cannot make people be kind to you, but you can allow the Holy Spirit to teach you how to be kind to other. Always be gentle and kind to one another.

Days 11 - 15

Rules to Gentleness (Kindness)

Scripture Text

Nehemiah 9:17

And refused to obey, neither were mindful of thy wonders that thou didst among them; but hardened their necks, and in their rebellion appointed a captain to return to their bondage: but thou art a God ready to pardon, gracious and merciful, slow to anger, and of great kindness, and forsookest them not.

The people of God were guilty of refusing to obey Him. They forgot about all the wonders God performed in their midst when He brought them out of bondage. The Lord provided for them with so much tender love and care, but this did not prevent them from walking away from Him. They became hard hearted and stiff necked against God, which led them into rebellion (active opposition to His authority).

While walking in rebellion they appointed a leader to lead them back into the bondage they came out of. The chosen people of God were walking in a bad and dangerous place in the presence of their loving and kind God. The Lord had promised them that He would never leave them, and they promised God that they would never leave Him, but they broke their promise. This is how they rewarded God for His provision for them.

But God, being the God He is, knew that the people needed something from Him that they could not get from any other place or individual. They needed to experience the pardoning (forgiving) powers of God, the gracious and merciful (unearned favor and compassionate) side of God. They also knew that God is slow to anger, full of great kindness (gentleness), and God would never leave them. God is always faithful to His word and to His promises, even when we are not.

Not only did God show kindness to them, but He is also giving His great kindness to you today. With the Holy Spirit abiding inside of you, God is providing constant care and great kindness. Knowing what you know about the history of the chosen people of God and how they walked contrary to the will of God, should push you to walk in Holy Respect to God and show kindness to others.

There are certain rules to kindness that will enable you to be all that God purpose in your life:

1) - Always show great kindness to everyone in need whether they are able to return the kindness or not (Acts 28:2 - And the barbarous people shewed us no little kindness: for they kindled a fire, and received us every one, because of the present rain, and because of the cold). The apostle Paul and many others had been shipwrecked and needed help. The people of the island they came upon, were very kind to them and gave them such things as they needed. We are required to do the same. They were not Christians, but they showed kindness. If they could be kind without the Spirit of God, how much more should Christians walk in kindness? There is no excuse for being rude and unkind to others.

2) - Christians must always make every effort to live like Jesus. You must use every effort to walk in kindness and gentleness (Colossians 3:12 - Put on therefore, as the elect of God, holy and beloved, bowels of mercies, kindness, humbleness of mind, meekness, longsuffering). Because you have been elected by God, you are to put on kindness. Because you are holy and beloved of God, you must put forward all that is within you to walk in the kindness of our Lord Jesus Christ. This should be an everyday walk for you, without thinking about it.

3) - Your speech should reflect kindness to all people. Whenever you open your mouth, the wisdom of God should flow freely with kindness written all over your words (Proverbs 31:26 - She opened

her mouth with wisdom; and in her tongue is the law of kindness). Whenever you open your mouth to speak, because wisdom comes from God, your words should display that you have been with God. Kindness must flow from your heart because it is a fruit of the Spirit. Christians should not be connected to cruel and harsh actions and speech! These are some of the areas in your life that needs much attention when it comes to gentleness and kindness. As you allow the Lord to move in your heart regarding your spiritual gift of gentleness, be mindful of how you handle, talk, and do charity for others starting this week.

***This is week three! Proceed with the kindness of the Holy Spirit from your heart. Do not just talk kindness but mix it into your daily walk.

Remember, that God do not look at your outward display, but He looks at your heart. What's in the secret parts of your heart?

Days 16 - 20

Gentleness Really Cares

Scripture Text

Romans 12:10

Be kindly affectioned one to another with brotherly love; in honor preferring one another.

This Scripture is talking about the Christian's conduct. You are to be kindly affectionately one to another. Your conduct must reflect the same conduct as Christ gave and taught to His disciples. We have been given the Spirit of God to walk inside of us making it possible to live this life of kindness. It does not matter how mean or hateful you were before Christ, the new you (born again) is to walk in the newness of life daily, with kind affections towards others. The Holy Spirit gives you the power to be kindly affectionate to others.

This is not limited to Christians only, but to everyone. When kindness is who you are, it will happen to all. It will not be an imposition on your part because this is the real you. Many people find it hard to show kindness to others even after becoming a Christian. But the truth is, you must realize that the Holy Spirit will help you change, if and only if, you allow Him to do His part. He was sent to do specific things in your life, but your were also instructed to allow Him to have His way in your life. So, if you are always leading, the Holy Spirit will never be allowed to complete His mission in you. Stop leading and start following the Holy Spirit directions. Learn how to submit to God's authority through the Holy Spirit.

You are commanded to love others with brotherly love and in honor, prefer one another, meaning to give more priority to others above yourself. This can only happen through the help of the Holy Spirit.

It does not mean that you are not important to God, but it helps to break away pride and selfishness from your heart. Kindness allows you to experience a closeness to one another and you will also develop mutual respect in your relationship. The fruit of gentleness is awesome, it can transform your character. Do you welcome this change?

1) - Gentleness will teach you how to have sympathy and empathy for others. You will not have to think about doing this, it will naturally happen because of who you are in Christ Jesus (Romans 12:15 - Rejoice with them that do rejoice, and weep with them that weep). When a heart has been filled with the kindness and gentleness of God, what you are made of inside will surely come out of you naturally. From your heart you will respond correctly to each circumstance that presents itself. Please know that others will know if your are real in your kindness.

2) - Gentleness will remove the hardness from your heart and replace it with gentle ways of helping other when they need your help (2Peter1:7-8 - [7)]-And to godliness brotherly kindness; and to brotherly kindness charity. [8)]-For if these things be in you, and abound, they make you that ye shall never be barren nor unfruitful in the knowledge of our Lord Jesus Christ). Brotherly kindness will produce love in you and if these things stay inside of your heart, you will always be fruitful in gaining the knowledge of Christ. The more you learn and develop kindness towards others, the more you will walk and become like Jesus Christ your Lord. Make this a priority in your walk as a Christian.

3) - When you live a life of gentleness you will give others the permission to walk in kindness also (Philippians 3:17 - Brethren, be followers together of me, and mark them which walk so as ye have us for example). When gentleness really cares, you will see others trying to follow your lead in being kind to others. Sometimes people are not familiar with showing kindness to others and some may even think that gentleness is a sign of weakness. But because you walk in kindness, they will see that being kind and gentle does not mean that you are weak. The results will only prove that you are strong in Jesus Christ.

***This week, allow yourself to walk in a way showing that gentleness really cares for others. Do not be afraid to allow your fruit of gentleness to flourish and make you more productive in Christ Jesus. Depend on The Holy Spirit to have His way.

Remember, do not hold back on showing kindness in every situation you encounter this week. It will only mature your fruit, not cripple you!

Days 21 - 25

Choose to be Gentle

Scripture Text

Ephesians 4:32

And be ye kind to one another, tenderhearted, forgiving one another, even as God for Christ's sake hath forgiven you.

In this full passage of Scripture, Paul the apostle, is alerting the Church of Ephesus of the difference between the old life they once lived and their new life in Christ Jesus. He tells them to pull off the old way of living and to be renewed in the spirit of their mind. He informs them that the new man is created in righteousness and true holiness after God Himself. To start the process of change in their lives, they had to renew their mind. The Holy Spirit is already living in your heart.

The Christians are instructed to put away all of the evil works of their flesh (old man and old way of living) and walk in the newness of life in the Spirit of God (in holiness and righteousness). Then Paul goes on to say to the Church: **1)-to be kind one to another, 2)-to be tender hearted, and 3)-to forgive one another.** Why would He give such a message to the Church, and what is the reasoning behind this message?

The apostle Paul gave such instructions to the Church, because God, for Christ's sake had forgiven them. They must show in their lives the same kindness to one another as they walk with Jesus the Son of God. They must choose to be kind and show kindness to one another. This is a command, but one must make the choice to obey what is instructed. You still have freedom of choice in Christ.

1) - You must choose to be gentle to one another from your heart. It does not matter how many times you read and talk about it, if it is not in your heart, you will not perform the action (Proverbs 16:9

- A man's heart deviseth (plans) his way: But the Lord directeth his steps). If you are going to plan your way, plan to be kind to one another from your heart, then the Lord will direct your steps in that direction. You must understand that God is in control of your life, and He will direct your steps if you will choose and allow Him to do so. The Holy Spirit is waiting for you to agree with Him to mature your fruit of kindness. Work with the Spirit and become mature.

2) - You must choose to be tenderhearted (compassionate) to one another. Kindness will teach you to be compassionate to others (1Peter 3:8 - Finally, be ye all of one mind, having compassion one to another, love as brethren, be pitiful, be courteous). As you respond to others in the spirit of kindness you will began to show compassion to people when it is needed. Please believe that others will see your compassion toward people, and will learn how to produce the same Christian conduct. Gentleness is an awesome virtue, and it is such an important quality to possess.

3) - Choose to forgive one another even if you are not the one at fault. Scripture teaches you that if you do not forgive others, your heavenly Father will not forgive you (Matthew 6:14-15 - 14)-For if ye forgive men their trespasses, your heavenly Father will also forgive you: 15)-But if ye forgive not men their trespasses, neither will your Father forgive your trespasses). Forgiving men their trespasses is an important act of pardoning on your part, it is the kindness from your heart that produces the action. Not only does it help the individual who is being pardoned, but you are also giving God permission to forgive your trespasses. This is how kindness from the heart works, forgive and be forgiven.

The Holy Spirit will always be there to guide you into doing the right things in your life with Christ. Please utilize the help that is provided for you. Stop trying to go at it alone, because you will not mature the fruit without the help of the Holy Spirit. After all He is the owner of the fruit. Please use your owner's manual (the Bible). Do not take long to think about this because you may talk yourself out of it. Listen to the voice of the Holy Spirit and allow Him to lead you.

***Take this week to make better choices when faced with opportunities to show kindness, compassion, and forgiveness to others.

Remember, you purpose kindness in your heart and the Holy Spirit will help you to mature the fruit of gentleness.

Days 26 - 30

Walking daily in Gentleness (Kindness)

Scripture Text

Galatians 5:22a

But the fruit of the Spirit is love, joy, peace, longsuffering, gentleness.

The fruit of the Spirit is **Gentleness.** We have learned a lots about gentleness this month, but now I would like to take the time to reinforce the need of having maturity in this fruit.

We are living in a time when gentleness is so rarely encountered when interacting with others. People from all walks of life seem to be so discouraged, stressed, disheartened, and some just plain mean and angry. Gentleness, compassion, and kindness, seems to be fading away. This is why Christians must live their life in gentleness daily. You must continue to walk as Jesus did with His disciples, showing gentleness and compassion to all. The world cannot afford to allow this great virtue to vanish from society. We must never stop caring for one another.

The Holy Spirit has not lost His ability to mature the fruit of gentleness in the believer's life. He is constantly waiting for you to ask for His help to grow spiritually. You cannot become numb to the need to be compassionate and empathetic to others. I know it is so demanding sometimes but the Church must still rise up to the call for gentleness and compassion.

As a Christian, when you encounter hardness from others, please react with gentleness. When you are wronged, please try to be kind. When things are going bad for you, please allow the Holy Spirit to comfort you, as you continue to be gentle. Do not turn callous (emotionally hardened, unfeeling, toughened) because others are hard. Keep praying and obeying the directions of the Holy Spirit and you will find yourself maturing in the fruit department of gentleness.

We are empowered by God through His Spirit to deal differently with others (Colossians 3:12 - Put on therefore as the elect of God, holy and beloved, bowels of mercies, kindness, humbleness of mind, meekness, longsuffering). People need to be loved, and the true trademark of love is to show kindness, compassion, gentleness, sympathy, and empathy. Without these being present in the church, communities, and in the believer's life, where would the world find help?

Gentleness cares for the feelings of others, shows compassion when someone else needs it. Gentleness do not have to be treated gentle, for it to respond in the correct way. Yes, there will be times when you may not respond properly, but this should not happen every day in the believer's life. You must mature to a point where gentleness, compassion, and kindness is what you do because of who lives in you. Practicing this daily, will make kindness reach perfection.

When others are suffering on any level, your gentleness should prompt you to share in the process with them. You should not have to think long and hard about what to do, if your fruit is maturing. Just do it!

Believers are to be kind to one another in brotherly love. Many times, you find people able to show kindness and compassion to others, but forget to show the same virtue to their brothers and sisters in Christ. Do not take one another for granted! Just because you are all Christians, be careful not to lose your compassion in the House of God. **This can happen if you stop being concerned for one another (Romans 12:10 - Be kindly affectioned one to another with brotherly love; in honour preferring one another).** Keep the gentle spirit thriving in the Church and walk in it when and wherever you go. Keep the love of God flowing between you and others, so that the Spirit of God will have the type of unity needed, to mature your spiritual fruit of gentleness.

***This week, do not allow things to come between you and others that will cripple your relationship as brethren in the Lord.

Remember, to reflect on the way you are to respond to others with your fruit of gentleness. Make maturing this fruit a top priority in your life.

NOTES

Month Nine - Maturing the Fruit of Goodness

Days 1 - 5

What is Goodness?

Scripture Text

Romans 15:14

And I myself also am persuaded of you, my brethren, that ye also are full of goodness, filled with all knowledge, able also to admonish one another.

This is a letter from the apostle Paul to the Roman Churches. He had not met them yet. He was persuaded in his heart that they were all full of goodness and filled with all knowledge of the basic truth of the Gospel of Jesus Christ. He knew they were Christians just as he was. The condition of Paul's heart and his love and respect for the Spirit of God, made him sure that the people of God were full of the virtues of God. Goodness is a virtue!

Goodness means being full of excellence, kindness, virtue, and helpfulness; the state or quality of being good. Because goodness is one of the spiritual fruit given to every believer, the goodness of God rest inside of you. When the goodness of God is inside of you, goodness is what you do. You will walk in goodness every day. As this fruit matures, goodness will become so natural for you to perform.

Paul trusted the power of God in every Christian's heart, to fill them with His goodness and knowledge. If God could do it for him, he was sure God did the same for the Christians in the Roman Churches. The Churches had been growing for some time, and Paul knew that growth could only happen, if they were able to teach and instruct people in the things of Jesus Christ. He was very confident that God's Spirit was the guiding force to their success. Paul understood the process of spiritual maturity in Jesus Christ.

Knowing the goodness of God, Paul also knew the people were able to admonish (caution, warn, remind of obligations) one another. There must be a balance in the goodness, knowledge, and admonition in the Church. One without the other will not be very effective in producing great spiritual maturity.

1) - Goodness is not being happy all the time, as some would think. It is having a good heart, full of righteousness and truth, loving and treating others the way you desire to be treated (Ephesians 5:9 - For the fruit of the Spirit is in all goodness, and righteousness and truth). You are delivered from the life of darkness and sin, now you are filled with the powerful Spirit of the Living God, and He is full of GOODNESS. Now that goodness has filled your heart, it is absolutely necessary that you live and walk as who you are meant to be in Christ Jesus.

2) - From your heart the goodness of God will speak the truth at all times, whether it is painful or rewarding (Psalm 119:30 - I have chosen the way of truth: thy judgments have I laid before me). When the spiritual fruit of goodness is in your heart, you will purpose to speak truth at all times. Truth may not agree with popular options, but it is righteousness and goodness. Speak the truth in all things. Keep this as part of your eternal purpose, do not move away from this. Goodness should always be used in every action and duty you perform, in caring for others. Always remind yourself that you are dealing with God's people, and He will reward you for how you handled them whether good or bad.

***This is week one of the spiritual fruit of goodness. Take your time this week to get familiar with this fruit and what you need to do concerning the teachings. Starting with truth and righteousness let us walk it out.

Remember, the Holy Spirit is available to help you in these areas, just ask for the help you need.

Days 6 - 10

See Good and Just Do it

Scripture Text

Ephesians 2:10

For we are His workmanship, created in Christ Jesus unto good works, which God hath before ordained that we should walk in them.

In this Scripture, we are reminded of the fact that we are created (new creatures) in Christ Jesus to do good works. We are no longer obligated to do the sinful work of our past life in sin. We are now to live a life of goodness. Performing good works unto all people. These good works have been ordained (established, appointed, set, or decreed) of God that you must walk in them. This is a requirement of God for the new you. Get ready for your change!

In the beginning of this passage of Scriptures, Paul was teaching the Christians about the way they once walked, before accepting Jesus as their personal Savior. Then he goes on to tell them that the behavior they once displayed was alright, because they were sinners. But God through His grace and mercies, has given the believers His Spirit to enable them to live in the newness of life and walk in the goodness of God. There is no excuse for not walking in goodness.

1) - You must learn how to humble yourself unto God so that He can produce in you the heart you need, to walk in goodness. Yes, you received the fruit of goodness with the Holy Spirit, but you must allow Him to mature this fruit in you (Ephesians 5:9 - For the fruit of the Spirit is in all goodness and righteousness and truth). As you mature in righteousness, your spiritual fruit must also mature to help you walk out what you know about Christian living. The only way to learn how to do this is to practice it daily, until you finally get it.

2) - When you see good that needs to be done, please do not stand by and wait for someone else to do it (2 Corinthians 9:8 - And God is able to make all grace abound towards you; that ye, always having all sufficiency in all things, may abound to every good work). If you are the one to see it, take the initiative to do it. Please have the right attitude when you are performing whatever it is that needs to be done. You cannot say that you are full of goodness and whenever the situation presents itself, you keep walking by. To have goodness is to do goodness! Stop walking away from the need and walk up to it. Never feel like you are doing more than someone else because you are doing what is good. God will pay you for what you do. Keep being and doing good to everyone.

3) - When you perform good works, you bring glory to God. It shows that you are not all about yourself, but concerned about the good of others (1Peter 2:12b -Whereas they speak evil against you as evildoers, they may by your good works, which they shall behold, glorify God in the day of visitation). Even when people speak evil against you, and you continue to do good and show goodness towards them, they will begin to bring glory to God. People will take notice of the virtue in you because you are not rendering evil for evil, but good when evil is being done unto you. Keep walking in the fruit of goodness and watch your fruit mature. It is so important that the world see the fruit of goodness in operation in the Christian's life. It will show them that goodness is still being fruitful and multiplying in the earth, through the people of God.

***This week work on goodness to overcome evil. Do not focus so much on how bad you are treated, but on the opportunity, you have been given to bring glory unto God. So, whenever you see the opportunity to do good or goodness, just do it!

Remember, bringing glory to God is what you are meant to do and walking in goodness will make it happen.

Days 11 - 15

Depart From Evil and Do Good

Scripture Text

Titus 3:8

This is a faithful saying, and these things I will that thou affirm constantly, that they which have believed in God might be careful to maintain good works. These things are good and profitable unto men.

Being good or showing goodness some of the time is not enough. You, as a Child of God must walk in goodness everyday because it is of profit to you and to others. Paul was reminding Titus of the need to affirm (to declare positively or firmly) constantly, that the believer's should be very careful to keep doing good works. They are not to stop because they got tired, but to continue and they will profit from the results.

You may not see how you will profit from this at first, but as you continue to maintain good works, you will notice that you are not so easily moved by every situation. This is how your fruit starts to rise up in you and help you walk it out. This is how you will know that your fruit is actually maturing.

Many times, you may grow weary and tired because it seems the more you show goodness to others, the more they keep trying you. If you trust and rely on the Holy Spirit, He will direct your course and tell you how to handle every situation. A warning is necessary at this point **"Do not over ride the Holy Spirit".** The reason for this warning is, when you are mistreated, you may have the tendency to strike back especially when you are fed up. This is why you must allow the Holy Spirit to mature your spiritual fruit of goodness. **Listen, Listen, Listen to Him!**

1) - You cannot fight or control others because of who they are and what they do. You are a Christian, God's goodness and mercy will

follow you all the days of your life (Psalm 23:6a - Surely goodness and mercy shall follow me all the days of my life). So, you can allow the Spirit to help you control your behavior. You are responsible for your own actions. After all, you must give an account of your behavior and not someone else. A mature fruit of goodness will keep you within the will of God, pertaining to how you are to treat and care for others. Stand firm on holy living and pleasing God at all costs. Allow goodness and mercy to follow you for the rest of your life.

2) - When you depart or resist evil, goodness will become a major part of who you are and what you do on a daily basis (Psalm 34:14 - Depart from evil, and do good; seek peace, and pursue it). In the process of departing from the evil, you must do good, seek peace in the situation, and pursue (to follow in an effort to overtake or capture, chase) it. Goodness is a spiritual heavyweight fruit, because as you do good to others, you must seek peace in the situation, and continue to chase after peace until you have captured it. Hold on to peace as you do good to others. Please know that when your peace is being disrupted, pay close attention to the leading of the Holy Spirit to see what is causing this disruption.

3) - It is the will of God that you follow after what is good and do not practice doing evil for evil (1 Thessalonians 5:15 - See that none render evil for evil unto any man; but ever follow that which is good, both among yourselves, and to all men). Sometimes people are not always kind and thoughtful, but this Scriptures speaks very boldly and loud to the Christians, commanding you not to render evil for evil to anyone. It does not matter if they are a Christian or not, He says to any man! God is saying to follow that which is good to everybody, no exception. Because you know what is good, you are responsible for performing what you know.

***I know what you have learned for this week is very deep, but it is not impossible. You must take this week to digest this word and allow the

Spirit of God to manifest it in your life. Maturity of this fruit is what you are seeking after.

Remember, God will not tell you to do anything that He knows you cannot perform! You can do this.

Days 16 - 20

Goodness is Discipline

Scripture Text

2 Thessalonians 1:11

Wherefore also we pray always for you, that our God would count you worthy of this calling, and fulfill all the good pleasure of His goodness, and the work of faith with power.

This Scripture teaches the importance of someone praying always for you. Apostle Paul is praying that God would count the believers worthy of the calling that God has called them to. Also, to complete or fulfill all the good pleasures of the goodness of God with power by faith. God requires you fulfilling your call in excellence, through the power of the Holy Spirit. Do not half do the assignment, always perform it in excellence. Always give it all you have from your heart.

You must note that no one is worthy to stand in the good pleasures of God, except by faith in the Lord Jesus Christ. To be counted worthy of the calling that God has called you to do, you must first walk in the Spirit of God, as being born again through the salvation plan of Jesus Christ. There is no other way to be counted worthy of being called of God, and to fulfill every good pleasure of God's goodness, except you follow His divine plan for your life.

All of your goodness comes from God because God is good. God is perfect, and to fulfill all of His good pleasures, you must be able to walk in His presence. This will only happen in the will of God. The will of God can only be fulfilled through His Son, Jesus Christ. We must know that none of us are good within ourselves.

1) - Jesus completed all of His Father's will in perfect goodness

and excellence. Now Jesus is the author and finisher of your faith (Hebrews 12:2 - Looking unto Jesus the author and finisher of our faith, who for the joy that was set before Him endured the cross, despising the shame, and is set down at the right hand of the throne of God). Because of what Jesus endured, you are now able to fulfill all of God's good pleasures in your life through faith with the power of God. Your faith started with Jesus, and it can only reach the finish line in Him.

2) - To walk worthy of God's calling, you must walk by the discipline of the Holy Spirit and stay the course. The Holy Spirit was sent to live inside of you to lead and guide you into all truths and righteousness (John 16:13 - Howbeit when he, the Spirit of truth, is come, he will guide you into all truth: for he shall not speak of himself; but whatsoever he shall hear, that shall he speak: and he will show you things to come). It takes discipline on the believer's part to obey the voice, directions, and will of the Holy Spirit. You cannot produce the kind of goodness that the Holy Spirit requires and gives to you. Why not discipline yourself to obey His leading for you? Walking in goodness requires discipline from you at all times. Obedience and goodness must be in you to finish your course.

3) - It is in the Christian's conduct to prove what is the good, acceptable, and perfect will of God. This is done through being transformed by renewing your mind (Romans 12:2 - And be not conformed to this world: but be ye transformed by the renewing of your mind, that ye may prove what is that good, and acceptable, and perfect will of God). It truly takes discipline to have a changed mind. You must allow the Holy Spirit to direct you on how to keep transforming your mind. You will need to keep doing good, over and over. The more you do good the more your mind will adjust to the changes. Continue in doing good daily and watch your spiritual fruit of goodness mature.

***Being good and living a life in goodness means that goodness and mercy follows you! When you allow goodness and mercy to follow you, there is no law against this.

Remember, to allow yourself to serve the Lord in goodness throughout this entire week and start the transformation for a changed mind.

Days 21 - 25

Joy in Goodness

Scripture Text

2 Corinthians 9:7-8

7)-Every man according as he purposeth in his heart, so let him give; not grudgingly, or of necessity: for God loveth a cheerful giver. 8)-And God is able to make all grace abound towards you; that ye, always having all sufficiency in all things, may abound to every good work.

In these Scriptures Paul is teaching the believers on how to give. He tells them that when they give, there is a certain behavior in which they should do it. You are to give as you purpose in your heart, wanting to do so but with a joyful heart **(do not try to do what others do and not to be seen of others).** This behavior is not just limited to giving monetary gifts. It is also important when you give your time to others in need, when you pray for others, when you show goodness to others, and when you do anything for someone else.

Goodness must always find its roots in your heart. If it is done any other way, it profits you nothing. When you give of yourself to others in acts of goodness, be careful of your motivations behind the services. Man may speak very highly of your doings, but the Almighty God looks at the condition of your heart. He and He alone knows the what, when, and how you gave of your services. Do not try to impress man, always seek to please God when you give. Make sure your heart is involved in all of your doings.

God loves a cheerful giver, and He will make grace abound **(increase greatly)** towards you. God is your provider, and He will make sure that you always have sufficiency in all things and that you will increase greatly in every good work. This is awesome information for every Christian. This is why you must have joy in your goodness. This is a matter of your heart.

1) - It is an honor to serve the Lord in goodness and gladness (Psalm 100:2a - serve the Lord with gladness). Some may call it weakness because they do not understand what you know about being a cheerful giver. When you are able to have gladness or joy in your heart while doing good for others, you are honoring God through your service. Keep on being a cheerful giver.

2) - The goodness of God should teach you to give with a willing mind, not the mind of boasting (2 Corinthians 8:12 - For if there be first a willing mind, it is accepted according to that a man hath, and not according to that he hath not). God will judge you by what you have and are able to give versus what you do not have and are not able to give. Do not broadcast what you do for others, because you will already have your reward. Find joy in giving from your heart. Only you and God knows just what you can do for and give to others. Work it out in your heart so that God will get the glory out of your goodness, from your heart.

3) - Joy is a fruit of the Spirit and it is so exciting to see how this gift works with the gift of goodness (Ephesians 5:9 - For the fruit of the Spirit is in all goodness and righteousness and truth). The fruit of the Spirit is in all goodness. Since joy is a fruit of the Spirit, you should be joyful in your serving with goodness. What a perfect team "Joy and Goodness". As you begin to understand more about the fruit of goodness, your fruit and your mind should mature together.

***Spend this week walking in the joy of the Lord while serving with goodness to others.

Remember, Joy in Goodness!

Days 26 - 30

Goodness in You is Forever

Scripture Text

Philippians 1:6

Being confident of this very thing, that he which hath begun a good work in you will perform it until the day of Jesus Christ.

Please say it with me **"Goodness Is with You Forever."** I know it may be hard for you to believe that goodness will be in you forever, but it really is true. You can be confident in God that He started a good work in you, and He will perform it until the day that Jesus Christ returns. Now that is forever!

Goodness is a fruit of the Spirit of God and since He lives inside of you, goodness is a part of you. You will have goodness abiding in you for the rest of your life. Therefore, you cannot make any excuses why you cannot treat other good. This is not the type of gift you pick up when you want it, and put it down when you feel like you do not need it. It is given to you as a virtue of the Holy Spirit.

You can choose not to use goodness, or you can choose to walk in this gift daily. Just as you can override the Holy Spirit by choice, you can do the same with His gift. The choice is totally up to you, but you will still have the gift inside of you. God will not take the gift from you, but you can choose not to use it.

Please do not make a habit of disobeying the Spirit of God because it can put you in dangerous places. When you refuse to be good to others, you send out the message that you are not a good servant of God. When you see good and you refuse to do whatever it is that needs to be done, you are refusing to walk in the Holy Spirit. Develop a sensitive ear to hear what the Spirit is saying to you.

1) - To keep refusing to obey God is sending Him the message that you really don't love Him, because to love God is to obey Him (Luke 6:46 - And why call ye me, Lord, Lord, and do not the things which I say). You cannot keep calling Jesus Lord and not obey Him. At some point you will either start obeying His will for you, or decide to walk away from His love. This will become your choice.

2) - Goodness will show that you are compassionate from your heart, because you help others even if you are not shown the same kindness (1John 3:17 - But whoso hath this world's good, and seeth his brother hath need, and shutteth up his bowels of compassion from him, how dwelleth the love of God in him? You cannot say you love God and refuse to help others when they truly need your help. It is great to ask yourself this question, what do you have that God did not give unto you? When you recognize that God is the only one who has everything he needs, you will see why you need to show goodness and compassion to others.

You may be the one who is doing great right now, because we are all humans and subject to the fact that all will suffer, show goodness and mercy to all people. It may be hard for you to process this type of living, but if you keep walking in the Holy Spirit, you will understand why it was absolutely necessary for your heart to change. God has to soften your heart to the heart that will please and honor Him, and not you always honoring yourself. This is breaking the selfishness out of you.

3) - Being selfish can be very toxic, the only way to get rid of it, is to be good and merciful to others as you love and obey God. As you begin to humble yourself under the mighty hand of God, He will exalt you in due time (1Peter 5:6 - Humble yourselves therefore under the mighty hand of God, that He may exalt you in due time). God is always faithful, and you will not lose your rewards. This will also alert you to the fact that you are maturing in the area of goodness.

***This is the last week of Goodness. As you continue to serve God in goodness, understand that being good to others is not a weakness but a strength. Anyone can be rude, nasty, and uncaring at anytime, but it take the love of God in your heart to care for God's people in God's way. Be thankful that God has placed the fruit of goodness inside of you and is willing to use you in this area of your life.

Remember, keep your heart in the spirit of goodness, kindness, and compassion at all times. When it is your time to be shown goodness, it will come back unto you (Ecclesiastes 11:1 - Cast your bread upon the waters: for thou shalt find it after many days).

NOTES

Month Ten - Maturing the Fruit of Faith

Days 1 - 5

What is Faith (Faithfulness)?

Scripture Text

Luke 19:15-17

15) - And it came to pass, that when he was returned, having received
the kingdom, then he commanded these servants to be called unto
him, to whom he had given the money, that he might know how
much every man had gained by trading. 16) - Then came the first,
saying, Lord, thy pound hath gained ten pounds. 17) - And he said
unto him, well, thou good servant: because thou hast been faithful
in a very little, have thou authority over ten cities.

This is the parable of a nobleman going into a far country, to receive a kingdom unto himself. Before leaving, he called his ten servants and gave them ten pounds (about three month wages) and told them to occupy until he comes back. The people of the city hated the nobleman and refused to honor him as the nobleman he was. But the nobleman still expected faithfulness from his servants. He expected them to work every day as if he were still there with them. It did not matter how everyone else felt about him, these were his servants and he required faithfulness from them.

Upon the nobleman's return, he called for his servants to give a full report of how they had managed his money while he was away. The first servant came in and told his master that the pounds he left in his care had gained ten pounds more. This servant was a perfect picture of faithfulness to his master. The nobleman was so pleased with the servant that he said unto him, well, thou good servant, because you were faithful over a little, he gave him authority over ten cities. The servant was greatly rewarded for his faithfulness to his master.

Faithfulness is required of every Christian as you walk with God! You are not to be faithful for a day and unfaithful the next day. You are the servant of God and faithfulness is expected from you even if no one else is faithful.

So, what is faithfulness?

Faithfulness means - being trustworthy, loyal, true, constant, fast, steadfast, staunch, Adhering firmly and devotedly, as to a person (the American Heritage College Dictionary).

Just as the master of those servants expected loyalty from them, so does your heavenly Father expect loyalty from you. Being trustworthy is very important in the life of a Christian. If you can be trusted with a little while you serve God, He will be able to place more authority in your hands later. Your reputation also rides on your being faithful. People will trust you according to your faithfulness.

1) - Faith (faithfulness) is a fruit of the Spirit and is given to each believer as a source of power to produce faithfulness to God (Galatians 5:22 - But the fruit of the Spirit is love, joy, peace, longsuffering, gentleness, goodness, faith). Just like the other fruit, it is a part of the Holy Spirit and can only be given by the infilling of the Holy Spirit. This is why you find many people unable to be faithful always. The Holy Spirit is the power who gives the believers the ability to be constant in faithfulness. This is not a work of your own, but the power of the Holy Spirit. There is no reason for you to boast or brag about how faithful you are, but to thank God for the power of His Spirit in you. Your responsibility is to allow the Holy Spirit to work in you. Again, the Holy Spirit leads and you must follow.

2) - In serving the Lord, you must learn how to deny yourself and trust God totally (Matthew 16:24 - Then said Jesus unto His disciples, if any man will come after me, let him deny himself, and take up his cross, and follow me). To come after God, you must be faithful and devoted to Him. You cannot faithfully follow Christ if you are always in your own way. Faithfulness teaches you self denial, and this is where your faithfulness plays a great part in your Christian walk every day. As you remove yourself from first place in your life, you give consent to God taking that top place as the head! Now you can take up your cross and follow Him. With God as your head you will become faithful in your Christian walk.

3) - God will never expect you to be faithful to Him if He were not faithful to you (1 Corinthians 1:9 - God is faithful, by whom ye were called unto the fellowship of His Son Jesus Christ our Lord). God is totally faithful to you and has given you of His Spirit to enable you to be faithful to Him. God is supplying the help you need to be faithful to Him. Let the Holy Spirit help produce in you total faithfulness. Your faithful God called you into fellowship with His Son Jesus Christ, now you can please, honor, and appreciate Him by being faithful unto Him. Please do not allow anything to keep you from maturing in your relationship with your Heavenly Father.

***Take this first week to refresh yourself on the need to be faithful to God. Also stir up the desire to be faithful in all areas of your life, by studying the word of God and rekindling your desire to be faithful.

Remember, your God is faithful, and He will not fail you!

Days 6 - 10

Loyalty to God in Faithfulness

Scripture Text

1 Corinthians 4:1-2

1) - Let a man so account of us, as the ministers of Christ, and stewards of the mysteries of God. 2) - Moreover, it is required in stewards, that a man be found faithful.

Christians have been given an awesome called to walk as ministers of the Most High God. For this reason alone, you should be found faithful and loyal to your God and His call in your life. Always remembering that He could have called someone else, but instead He chose you. Every Christian is a minister on one level or another, so do not say this is not for you. It is exactly for you if you are a believer of Jesus Christ. We are all servants of the Most High God.

As a minister of God, Paul was saying to let a man give account or testimony of his stewardship, as to how he handled the Gospel and mysteries of God. He knew that God required that a man be found faithful in all he did for Christ. Paul took his relationship with God very serious, and it showed by the way he walked.

Being loyal to God is what you are living for. When you came to Christ, faith was required, now that you are in Him, faith (faithfulness) is still required. Every day in the life of a Christian requires some level of loyalty and faithfulness. Since you belong to God, your alliance should always be to God and His will no matter what is going on in your life. Your circumstances should not dictate your faithfulness to God.

Paul wanted the people who knew him, to give an account of how he handled the work of God. He knew the report of the people regarding his affairs would be good. Paul was faithful and loyal to the God he served.

You must have the same interest in pleasing God through faithfulness and being true to Him.

1) - Loyalty is something you do not see very much of when it comes to the work of God, in or out the Church. You should have a deep devotion and an attachment to God as you grow in Him (Matthew 19:27a - Then answered Peter and said unto Him, Behold, we have forsaken all, and followed thee). The disciples of Jesus were so loyal to Him, they left everything to follow Jesus. They did all of this by faith and never lost their rewards. All of them had many issues in life, but they were still loyal to their master. Can you say without doubt that you are loyal to your Lord? How much are you willing to give up to follow Jesus? They gave up all to follow Him.

2) - Jesus was loyal to His Father and He honored their relationship by obeying everything God wanted Him to do (John 8:29 - And He that sent me is with me: the Father hath not left me alone; for I do always those things that please Him). Loyalty always produces obedience to God. Jesus did everything His Father instructed Him to do, because of His loyalty and love for Him. You belong to God, and He has done the most wonderful thing for you in giving you eternal life. Is this not enough to give Him total loyalty in everything? Loyalty is included in faithfulness. You cannot be faithful if you are not loyal. Obedience is a trademark of loyalty and every Christian must walk in loyalty and faithfulness at all times.

3) - When you are given an assignment from the Lord, your loyalty to Him will convince you to complete the work (Matthew 19:26 - But Jesus beheld them, and said unto them, with men this is impossible; but with God all things are possible). Loyalty will take you to the finish line even if you do not think you can make it. Some of your assignments may seem impossible, but your loyalty to God will tell you to trust God and let Him make it happen. All things are possible to Him who believes. Keep in mind that God will not give you any assignments that you are not able to complete.

***Take this week to reflect on your level of loyalty to God. Think about the things you could do to become more loyal to Him. Also find out what is it that's holding you back from walking in loyalty to Christ.

Remember, to become faithful you must also be loyal!

Days 11 - 15

Steadfast and Unmovable in Your Faithfulness

Scripture Text

1 Corinthians 15:58

Therefore, my beloved brethren, be ye steadfast, unmovable, always abounding in the work of the Lord, forasmuch as you know that you labour is not in vain in the Lord.

This is an encouragement given by the apostle Paul to the Corinthian Church. He was telling them to be steadfast and unmovable in their faithfulness and work for the Lord. He wanted them to know that whatever they did for God would not go without being rewarded. God is faithful to all of His promises, and to doubt that God would not hold up His word, would cause them to lose hope. If they lost their hope in Christ, nothing else would matter in life. **Never, ever, lose your hope!**

You are encouraged to know the same thing concerning your God. If God said it, please believe that it will come to pass. You may have cause to doubt others regarding the things they may promise you, but God is not like man. God cannot lie, so if He promises something, it will happen! Just do your part, knowing that God's part is already done.

God has everything in His possession that is needed, to make His will happen in your life. If He needs to move things from one place to another to bring you to His expected end, He can do that without any problems because He is ALMIGHTY GOD! Your God is the owner of the entire universe and can do whatsoever He pleases at any time, without the consent of anyone.

Please do not try to figure out how you will get rewarded for your faithfulness. This is all God's business, and you cannot figure it out. Just trust Him to make it happen.

1) - Being steadfast means to continue with God to the end. Just as you started with God, stay with Him (Philippians 1:6 - Being confident of this very thing, that He which hath begun a good work in you will perform it until the day of Jesus Christ). I know there are times when it may seem that you will not make it.

because things can get very hard. But studying the Word of God will give you the assurance you need to hang on in there. Do not throw your hands up to give up, if anything, throw your hands up to surrender everything unto the Lord. God started a good work in you, and He will complete what He started. God will not fail you, just remain steadfast in all you are doing for God.

2) - When talking about being unmovable, you are to stand with the persuasion that you will not be moved (Proverbs 12:3 - A man shall not be established by wickedness: But the root of the righteous shall not be moved). Like a large rock that has been in place for a long time, it is not easily moved. Even when pressure is applied, it still stands. You may even break it into pieces, some of it will still remain because it is steadfast. You are not to be easily moved off of Jesus, the Solid Rock. The example of super glue comes to my mind. Have you ever had something you treasured for a long time, break? You knew taping it back together would destroy the beauty of the object, so you used clear super glue and it was restored back to the original beauty. This is what it means to be steadfast in God. You may become broken, crushed, or maybe badly bruised, just know that if you stay with God, He will restore you back to wholeness again. Do not be moved! Your ashes can be turned into beauty if you allow the Holy Spirit to rule in your heart.

3) - You are to always abound (increase) in the work of the Lord, this calls for steady production in your assignment and knowledge of Christ (2 Peter 1:8 - For if these be in you, and abound, they make you that ye shall neither be barren nor unfruitful in the knowledge of our Lord Jesus Christ). If you remain steadfast and unmovable in the Lord, you will be sure to produce fruitfulness in all seasons of your life. You may not feel or see the production, but you will never be barren nor unfruitful in the knowledge of Jesus Christ. Stand on everything you know about God, and allow the Holy Spirit to solidify your walk and relationship in Jesus Christ. You can do this because of who lives in you. Always know that you do not trust God by your feelings, but by faith. The just shall live by faith!

***This week make a point of being steadfast in the Lord. If trouble comes your way, stand like a rock and make up in your mind, that you will not move off of what you know about God's faithfulness. God is always unchangeable.

Remember, nothing happens in your life without God knowing about it.

Days 16 - 20

Being Constant and Staunch in God

Scripture Text

Colossians 1:23

If ye continue in the faith grounded and settled and be not moved away from the hope of the gospel, which ye have heard, and which was preached to every creature which is under heaven; whereof I Paul am made a minister.

You must continue in the faith being grounded and settled. Do not be moved away from the gospel, was Paul's way of telling the Christians to be Constant (persistent, unchanging) and Staunch (firm, true). They had heard the gospel, and it was preached to everyone the way God told Paul to preach it. So now he wanted them to keep being persistent in what the word of God says.

Being a minister of God, from experience, Paul knew the only way people would be delivered and saved from their sins, would be through the true gospel of Jesus Christ. Therefore, he encouraged the Colossians to be grounded and settled (firm and established), also persistent and unchanging (constant), in the word of God. They are to never change the gospel to fit the people, but to keep the word of God pure and holy, even if the pure truth is not popular to the people.

1) - Being constant in the word of God and in the faith, means to stay persistent no matter what happens in your life. It means sacrificing your will, for the good of others and the will of God (Matthew 7:17 - Even so every good tree bringeth forth good fruit: but a corrupt tree bringeth forth evil fruit). You are not to change your morals or values from who you are in Christ, when it comes to the will and things of God. You must prove to yourself and to the people who are following your examples, that the word of God is always true, and it will accomplish everything Jesus said it would do. If your examples are faulty, who wants to follow you? Be sound and firm in your beliefs because you and only you know what the Lord has done for you and in you. **You know the power of "The Word of God".** Walk as one who has learned and is still learning of God and His ways. The knowledge of Jesus Christ is so powerful, so keep reading and studying His word to get to know Him better.

2) - Being firm and established in the faith is being rooted and grounded in the teachings of our Lord Jesus Christ (Colossians 2:7 - Rooted and built up in Him, and stablished in the faith, as ye have been taught, abounding therein with thanksgiving). You have not been given the authority to change the word of God. Therefore, you are to stand firm and establish yourself in whatever the word of God is saying. Paul stood on the word of God without wavering, even when his life was threatened. This is the same firmness required by every Christian. You are to stand firm in the word of God, in the Spirit of thanksgiving. Remember you were called by God and not God called by you. **Stand Faithfully on the Word of God!** As you stand firm in the Truth, your roots will run deep, and your faithfulness will soar.

3) - You are called to make disciples, and this means making followers of Christ. You can either teach them to be like Christ by standing on the truth or dilute (water down) the word of God, and they will not be like Him (Matthew 12:33 - Either make the tree good, and his fruit good; or else make the tree corrupt, and his fruit corrupt: for the tree is known by his fruit). What you do for Christ will last forever, if you do it the way you are instructed to do. Do not take upon yourself the responsibility to handle the Scriptures as you please. This can destroy many people's life, and yours as well. This teaching from Paul is worth heeding, because it is time for the people of the Most High God, to stand like a rock in their charge, convictions, and commitment to Him. Be constant and firm in what you are doing, and the Holy Spirit will give you the power and ability to bring glory to the name of the Lord. If you faithfully stand up on the truth, the truth will faithfully stand up in you, setting you and others free.

***This week take the time to reevaluate yourself to see how firm and persistent you are in your walk with the Lord. You can never be too committed to Jesus Christ.

Remember, if you want your fruit to remain, please stand on the truth of God's word! Stand like a ROCK, while standing on the ROCK "JESUS CHRIST"!

Days 21 - 25

Faithfulness in Obedience Brings Benefits

Scripture Text

Philippians 4:9

Those things, which ye have both learned, and received, and heard, and seen in me, do: and the God of peace shall be with you.

In this passage of Scripture, the Christians are instructed to do the things which they had learned, received, heard, and seen Paul do as a Minister, while serving God. For him to feel confident enough to tell them to follow him, he had to be living a well committed life for Jesus Christ. He also had to be obedient to God and living the kind of life God required of him.

Paul always put God first in his daily walk as an apostle. He understood quite well the charge that was laid upon him, and was dedicated to following the will of God without reservations. Whatever God told him to do, he did it. Wherever God told him to go, he went. He was able to complete assignments because of his faithfulness in obedience to his God. He knew the value of being faithful and obedient to the Lord from his heart. His service was not lip service, but action.

Faithfulness comes from trusting God with all your heart. Once you trust God from the heart, obedience is what you do. Putting the two together, you have a Christian with great confidence in his/her God. This type of relationship with God brings great benefits to your life. You will not become arrogant but confident in Jesus Christ.

1) - When you take the time to learn of God and his will, God will give you rest unto your soul (Matthew 11:29-30 - 29)-Take my yoke upon you, and learn of me, for I am meek and lowly in heart: and ye shall find rest unto your souls. 30)-For my yoke is easy and my burden

is light). When you learn of Christ, you will find out that He is meek and lowly, mild and gentle, and he is longsuffering and patient. He knows that life will happen, and hardship will be a part of every individual's life. Christ wants to place His yoke, His life, and His purpose upon you because it will fit you perfectly. He knows who you were meant to be and what you were purposed to complete in this life. You will also find rest for your soul. Everyone was not meant to weather the same storms in life. God knows exactly how to perfectly fit you into the place he has for you, and it will bring purpose, direction, and contentment into your life. If you have learned of Christ and really understood how much He loves you, you will understand the purpose of taking His yoke upon you. This is one of the benefits of faithfulness in obedience. Finding rest is what you were meant to do, and it will only happen by faithfully obeying and walking with and in Jesus Christ.

2) - When you hear and receive with a humble mind and a tender heart the word and the teachings of God, it can save your soul (James 1:21b - And receive with meekness the engrafted word, which is able to save your soul). Hearing the word of God is one thing. Hearing and receiving the word with a humble mind and tender heart, will cause you to have the fertile soil needed, to produce action to what you heard. This action should promote the right temperature in your heart for repentance and receiving God's plan of salvation. This is another benefit of faithfulness in obedience. You must hear, receive by faith, and obey the word of God to obtain eternal salvation. This is not only an earthly benefit, but this one is also eternal because of salvation. What a working and retirement benefit plan!

3) - Scripture teaches us to follow after righteousness. This is doing the examples of what is written and done by Jesus Christ. Paul told the Philippians to follow him as an example of following Christ (Philippians 3:17 - Brethren, be followers together of me, and mark them which walk so as ye have us for an example). Paul knew how he walked with Christ, and was confident that if others would follow him and imitate others who also lead by examples, there would be great benefits in Christ. God always have someone who is living the life they often speak of in Christ Jesus. Everyone is not half stepping in their relationship with the Lord. These are the Christians you should seek after and follow their examples. They would be able to help inspire you to stay faithful and obedient to the call of God. **Follow Christ, and as your leader, follow me only as I follow Christ.**

This week challenge yourself to learn, receive, hear, and seek after being faithful and obedient to God in all you do. Purpose to study the Word of God more each day. Allow the Holy Spirit to teach you how to walk faithfully and obedient to God, daily. This is a challenge, go for it and be a conquer in Christ Jesus.

Remember, faithfulness in obedience will bring you great benefits!

Days 26 - 30

Staying Faithful to Finish the Course

Scripture Text

2 Timothy 4:7

I have fought a good fight, I have finished my course, I have kept the faith.

The apostle Paul had just finished giving Timothy His Charge to continue being faithful and committed to the work of God. Paul had served over thirty years in the Gospel of Jesus Christ (from A.D.36-66). He had done great missionary work throughout the areas and remained faithful in all God charged to his hands. His assignment was of great importance to him, and he faithfully stayed the course regardless of all he had to suffer. He treasured his service to the Almighty God, and knew in his heart how great it was to be chosen by God for service.

When Paul is talking about fighting, he was not using his fist or verbal challenges in a battle. He spoke of running in the spiritual race of life, competing for the price of eternity with Jesus Christ. **He knew that he would be a winner, if he stayed faithful to the call and played by God's rules (1 Corinthians 9:24 - Know ye not that they which run in a race run all, but one receiveth the prize? So run, that ye may obtain).** Just as rules are necessary in games of sport, so are they necessary in the race for eternal life. God is a God of order.

In sports you can actually mess up a few times and may still be given another chance. In the race of life, you only get one chance at it, so choose to follow Jesus Christ and give Him all that you have within you. There is no second chance to relive this life. You must walk it out with God being your Father, leading and directing your every move. Run this race of life in the power of the Holy Spirit and do it in faithfulness, knowing this is the only life you have been given.

Staying faithful to the charge of God in your life is worth more than you may ever know. It covers so many things in how you will actually fair in this life. Many times, you will have choices that can cause great setbacks in your future. If you are not faithfully acknowledging the Lord in all your ways, you will probably choose the wrong path **(Proverbs 3:6 - In all thy ways acknowledge Him, And He shall direct thy paths).** Trust God to lead you all the way.

How do you view your service to God? Do you see it as an awesome opportunity to be a part of what God is doing in the earth, or do you see it as being hard to live this way? Do you see it as always wanting something from God, and never really completing the things He gives you to do? Again, how do you see your service to your Almighty God?

Paul said he had finished his course, meaning he preached and taught the truth of the Gospel. He did not preach messages about himself, because he knew there was no power to save a soul in him. Therefore, he did not waste his time on selfishness, but treasured every moment he had been given to tell the world all about Jesus Christ. That is call pure faithfulness. Only a mature spiritual fruit of faith can produce such dedicated service to God. How mature is your spiritual fruit of faithfulness?

Staying faithful to finish your course will depend on how you view your relationship with God, and your call to His service. This is why you really need to mature your spiritual fruit of faithfulness. As this fruit matures, you will blossom in pleasing God **(Hebrews 11:6 - But without faith it is impossible to please Him: for he that cometh to God, must believe that He is, and that He is a rewarded of them that diligently seek Him).** Please keep this Scripture deep in your heart!

In the end of this Scripture Paul writes, "I have kept the faith". Paul could look back over his journey with Christ and see how he said yes to God's call by faith. He received his call with a heart of thanksgiving, because he knew how he fought against the Son of God, out of ignorance. But God still loved him and wanted to use him in the Gospel. Paul, out of respect, gratitude, and honor to God, took the time to separate himself from the world entirely, and turn unto the life of a Christian without hesitation. He continued the work of the ministry faithfully until the end of his earthly life.

Paul, because of his experience in the gospel, and faithfulness to God, was able to tell his minister, Timothy, to also fight the good fight of faith and lay hold on eternal life (1 Timothy 6:12 - Fight the good fight of faith, lay hold on eternal life, whereunto thou art also called, and hast professed a good profession before many witnesses). Just as an athlete conditions his heart, mind, and body to contend for the activity he/she wants to win, so must the Christians condition themselves to win the good fight of faith. This will happen by staying faithful to the course and mature the spiritual fruit of Faithfulness.

***This is the last week of maturing your spiritual fruit of faithfulness! Take the time to reflect back on everything you have learned this month. Do not get in a hurry but be dedicated to the process of maturing this great fruit. I pray for your maturity of this great fruit "FAITHFULNESS".

Remember, without faith it is impossible to please GOD. This is why maturing your faith is so very important.

NOTES

Month Eleven - Maturing the Fruit of Meekness

Days 1 - 5

What is Meekness?

Scripture Text

1 Peter 3:4

But let it be the hidden man of the heart, in that which is not corruptible, even the ornament of a meek and quiet spirit, which is in the sight of God of great price.

This Scripture is teaching about the value of a meek and quiet spirit. It is found in the hidden man of the heart. You will not find it in the outward appearance. Many people think that meekness is in the way they dress or look, but this is far from the truth. Meekness is a fruit of the Spirit, and it is found only in the heart where the Holy Spirit resides. As you walk in the meekness of the Holy Spirit, you will start to display changes in your outward appearance, but the fruit itself in located in the heart.

Peter was teaching the women not to spend all their time focusing on their outward appearance, but utilize their time working on the hidden man in the heart. He walked with Jesus during his ministry on earth, and heard many lesson taught by the master teacher on meekness. He understood the true meaning of meekness and how it was to be used in the life of the Christian.

What is meekness? Showing patience, humble, gentle, tender, mild, and considerate. It is also strength to discipline and control when needed, and doing it at the right time.

Because meekness is a spiritual fruit, to possess it, you must be born again, and have the Holy Spirit residing inside of you. The reason it is so hard for some people to show meekness to others, they do not have it on the inside. You cannot show something that you do not have. It must be in your heart.

This particular fruit has been misunderstood by many people, because they tend to see it as a sign of weakness, rather than for the strength it really is. Meekness is strong and whenever you meet someone operating in this great fruit, please know that they are strong. When someone can be patient, humble, gentle, tender, mild, considerate, and have strength to discipline with control, that is strength! Make no mistake, they are not weak.

Many people want to display things on the outside, so others will see it, but give little attention to the hidden inner man of the heart. Things you wear or place on the outside will perish with time. It is the hidden man of the heart who is dressed in the Holy Spirit, producing the spiritual fruit, and guiding the life of that Christian. This individual understands what meekness is truly all about.

I would like to take this time to define what each ingredient of MEEKNESS mean:

1) - Patience - Longsuffering; forbearance; the capacity to endure hardship, difficulty, or inconvenience without complaints. Patience emphasizes self-control and the willingness of the ability to tolerate delay.

2) - Humble - Marked by meekness or modesty in behavior, attitude, or spirit. Not arrogant or prideful.

3) - Gentle - Considerate or kindly in disposition; amiable and tender. Not harsh or severe; mild and soft. Easily managed or handled.

4) - Tender - Considerate and protective; Marked by or expressing gentle emotions; loving. Given to sympathy or sentimentality; soft.

5) - Mild - Gentle or kind in disposition or behavior.

6) - Considerate - Having or marked by regard for the needs or feelings of others.

7) - Strength to control and discipline - It is a strong state of mind, who wants justice and righteous acts to be done, not overlooking the evil but also considers the entire situation. Discipline with control at the right time.

When looking at all of what meekness consist of, how can you call it weakness?

***Use this week to familiarize yourself with this fruit. Then look into your heart and see how mature your fruit of meekness really is. Start applying all of these ingredients in your daily walk as the Christian you are.

Remember, meekness is a fruit of the Spirit, and you must work with the Holy Spirit to allow Him to mature it.

Days 6 - 10

Love in Meekness

Scripture Text

Ephesians 4:1-3

1)-I therefore, the prisoner of the Lord, beseech you that ye walk worthy of the vocation wherewith ye are called, 2)-With all lowliness and meekness, with longsuffering, forbearing one another in love; 3)-Endeavoring to keep the unity of the Spirit in the bond of peace.

In these Scriptures, the Christians are encouraged to walk or live worthy of the job God has called them to do. Not only are they to walk worthy, but do it in the spirit of meekness and longsuffering, forbearing (tolerant or patient with) one another in love. These three fruit of the Spirit are mentioned together in this Scripture, as ingredients to prepare you for a worthy walk in God.

Clearly seen, the fruit of longsuffering, meekness, and love, is working together, as you are instructed to walk worthy of the vocation to which you are called, by God. They are all needed to fulfill the call. Without them being present in your life, you will not get it done. This is why you must mature these fruit and stay within the control of the Holy Spirit, to keep them growing.

1) - To walk worthy is to allow the Holy Spirit to empower you with the humble, gentle, mild, considerate, and strong, fruit of the Spirit of meekness, as you encounter others in your day to day living (1 Peter 5:6 - Humble yourselves therefore under the mighty hand of God, that He may exalt you in due time). There is no way you will be able to get the work of God done, without the aid and leadership of the Holy Spirit. Meekness should be included in everything you do, and it must be in your heart. Just as Jesus walked in meekness, so must you. To walk this way is to rely on the Holy Spirit, and obey His powerful leadership.

You must recognize that if the Holy Spirit is full of power, then every fruit He provides is a strong fruit. There are no such thing as a weak fruit in Christ Jesus! So, change your mind as to how you see the fruit of meekness. It takes a lot of control to walk in meekness daily, and to respond to situations with the right temperature of mind.

2) - Longsuffering is also mentioned in this Scripture. It is needed with meekness to be able to weather whatever storms that may be stirring, when meekness is in action and kind words are needed (Proverbs 15:1 - A soft answer turneth away wrath: But grievous words stir up anger). Everyone is not kind and gentle, so when you are being kind, gentle, and tender to them, the situation may require patience. This is when the Holy Spirit will give you the patience and whatever you need to remain calm. But you must listen and obey Him as He Speaks. Your words can either diffuse the situation, or it can make the situation blaze like a wildfire. This is unity in the fruit.

3) - Meekness and longsuffering must be applied in the spirit of love, to produce the expected result of the Spirit of unity in the bond of peace (Ephesians 4:2 - With all lowliness and meekness, with longsuffering, forbearing one another in love). There is a reason to use these two fruit in love. It is to keep the Spirit of unity from being disrupted in the body of Christ. **Since love covers a multitude of sins, many things can be overlooked or dealt with in a humble way (1 Peter4:8 - And above all things have fervent charity (love) among yourselves: for charity shall cover the multitude of sins).** The patience that is needed to see this process through, will be present because of the three fruit working together in your heart, by the power and authority of the Holy Spirit. Do not be overly concerned about how the other individual treats you, just be sure you are walking worthy of the vocation that God has called you to walk.

***This week make sure, that as you walk in meekness, you are able to apply longsuffering in the situations and do it in the spirit of love.

Remember, that love shall cover the multitude of sins!

Days 11 - 15
Forgiveness in Meekness
Scripture Text
Ephesians 4:31-32

31)-Let all bitterness, and wrath, and anger, and clamor, and evil speaking, be put away from you, with all malice: 32)-And be ye kind one to another, tender hearted, forgiving one another, even as God for Christ's sake hath forgiven you.

The Apostle Paul is giving instruction to the Christians, regarding their new way of life. He telling them to let all bitterness (resentment, harshness), wrath (burst of anger, violent explosive temper), anger (a strong feeling of displeasure or hostility), clamor (arguing, fussing, quarreling, brawling), evil speaking, and malice (slander, hurtful, injurious speech) be put away for them. He wanted them to know, that there is no room for these types of behaviors in their new walk with Christ. Notice, he did not say stop these behaviors, he said for them to put it away from themselves. Get rid of all old behaviors and start walking in the newness of life. Once you have completed this phase you are now ready to forgive others.

You are to treat one another with kindness and be tender hearted while you are doing this. Kindness and tender heartedness is also known as meekness. Once you pull off the old garments of sinful behaviors, you can truly begin to treat one another with the kind of respect God requires of you.

1) -The Holy Spirit is the only one who can make all of this happen. You must be renewed in the spirit of your mind and put on the new man after God (Ephesians 4:23-24 - 23)-And be renewed in the spirit of your mind: 24)-And that ye put on the new man, which after God

is created in righteousness and true holiness). You are not able to do this on your own, but with the help of God, all things are possible to him who believes. Pull off the old sinful mind and put on the new spiritual mind. The new man will have the desire to walk after God, his Father, in righteousness and true holiness. This is the reason you must mature your spiritual fruit, so that you will become more and more like Jesus Christ every day. Do not worry, take one day at a time to learn how to live holy.

2) - The reason you must pull off the old and put on the new, is to be able to forgive one another, even as God for Christ sake has forgiven you (1 John 2:12 - I write unto you, little children, because your sins are forgiven you for His name's sake). It is so important that you always remember, that God forgave you for all of your sins, now every day you must forgive others just because you were forgiven. I do know that you may have days when you are just not feeling it, you must constantly read and study the word of God (Bible) on Scriptures pertaining to forgiveness. Do not settle for excuses within yourself as to why you cannot forgive. Always pray and ask the Lord for His help in this and all other matters when you are having trouble. Do not waste time on trying to walk it alone. There are spiritual fruit with the Holy Spirit, available to help in your time of need. Please utilize your Helper!

3) - When you are willing to forgive others, your Heavenly Father will be willing to forgive you (Matthew 6:14-15 - [14)]-For if ye forgive men their trespasses, your heavenly Father will also forgive you: [15)]-But if ye forgive not men their trespasses, neither will your heavenly Father forgive your trespasses). You are to forgive other as you desire your heavenly Father to forgive you. Not only are you to forgive them, you are to do it in the spirit of meekness, not out of an obligation, because it is in your heart. You may ask what if it is not in my heart? My answer to you would be, it is not forgiveness. True forgiveness comes directly from a heart that recognizes you are changed and the Holy Spirit lives inside of you. Now is the time to start allowing the Holy Spirit to teach you, through the word of God, how to forgive and move on with your life. The more you do not forgive, the more you are not forgiven. So, work on matters of your heart until you are able to forgive other the correct way.

***Make this a week of forgiving others in the spirit of meekness. Do it from your heart. Use less lip service and more heart action!

Remember, the Holy spirit is able to help you mature your spiritual fruit of meekness and teach you how to forgive from your heart!

Days 16 - 20

Restoration in Meekness

Scripture Text

Galatians 6:1

Brethren, if a man be overtaken in a fault, ye which are spiritual, restore such a one in the spirit of meekness; considering thyself, lest thou also be tempted.

This week we will take the time out, to discuss a familiar topic in the Church community, regarding helping others when they are overtaken in a fault. This Scripture specifically teaches us (brethren), if a man be overtaken in a fault (falls into temptation by surprise or not deliberately), the Christians who are in a spiritual mature walk with God, are to restore the person back into the faith and wholeness. This is to be done in the spirit of meekness and not as a judge!

This is not just meant for the ministers, but for all mature Christians. You are to take time out to work with the individual in tenderness, kindness, gentleness, and love. The reason being, you cannot judge the person, but consider the fact that you too are human, and the same thing could very well happen to you. Now this is spiritual mature behavior on your part.

One of the main reasons you need to mature the fruit of meekness, is because you may encounter situations like these as you walk with Christ. Operating in the spirit of meekness from your heart, will enable you to help others in ways you never thought possible. When you consider yourself and the fact that you could also be tempted, you will know to use meekness as required by the Lord.

To restore (katartizete - to set a joint back into place) is the number one goal to meet in this individual's life right now. You are to help join the person back into the relationship with Christ, and the rest of the body. This will only happen if you do it the way the Scripture teaches. There is power when operating in the spirit of meekness. You allow the individual to recognize the wrongdoing, repent of it, and start the process of restoration in his/her life.

1) - Restoring some one in the spirit of meekness, means that you are living and walking in the Spirit yourself (Galatians 5:25 - If we live in the Spirit, let us also walk in the Spirit). The way you handle situations in your life will speak volumes about how you really live from day to day. So, whenever you are confronted with these types of issues, you will know exactly how to respond. You will also remember that this person is your brother in Christ, and how much you love him/her. You will not only approach the individual in the spirit of meekness, but you will also find yourself praying for their restoration, not focusing on their faults and failures. This is where your maturity stand tall in your Christian walk. Mature the fruit and be an encouragement to others and not just living for yourself.

2) - Studying the word of God will take you out of your fleshly walk, and sustain you in the Spirit of God. It will give you the answers you need in the time it is needed (Proverbs 15:28 - The heart of the righteous studieth to answer: but the mouth of the wicked poureth out evil things). Study the word of God, to find the wisdom you need to perform the will of God. Every Christian must pursue the wisdom of God so that you will be able to give wisdom. You cannot give what you do not have. Wisdom is one of those things. It does not matter how much you talk about wisdom, if you do not know how to apply it to circumstances, you have done nothing. This wisdom must be applied with meekness, in order to help bring the person back to wholeness again. You walking in your fleshly ways, will not get it done. You must walk in the Spirit of God.

3) - There may be a time when a rebuke is needed to restore a person back to wholeness, but make no mistake, meekness is also needed

at this time (2 Timothy 2:25 - In meekness instructing those that oppose themselves, if God peradventure will give them repentance to the acknowledging of the truth). Meekness has the strength to discipline and control, it does it at the right time. You must be able to control the situation, discipline if needed, and do it all at the right time, as not to destroy a person. This type of wisdom will only come by the leading and guiding of the Holy Spirit. The individual must be informed of the severity of the action, but it must be done in a way that the person will repent and return back to the Lord. You must remember your goal is to help restore the brother and not to destroy.

***This week think about how you would handle someone who is overtaken in a fault, and how you would want someone to handle you for the same thing. Would you want them to use meekness or not?

Always remember, Meekness is not weakness, but strength. Use it wisely to help others, maybe someone else will use meekness when you are the one in need.

Days 21 - 25

Obedience in Meekness

Scripture Text

James 3:13

Who is a wise man and endued with knowledge amongst you? Let him shew out of a good conversation his works with meekness of wisdom.

Obedience is needed in meekness, when you are instructing others in the ways of God. To instruct someone in the will of God, you must allow the Holy Spirit to instruct you first. To be effective in what you are instructing, you must be the first obedient partaker of what you want others to do or learn. If you have not learned it yet, please do not try to teach it. If you are not able to obey what you are instructing others to obey, please, by all means, keep it to yourself until you can perform it. It will be received better when you can perform it.

James is saying, if you are a wise man, and you know that God has blessed you with wisdom and knowledge for and among His people, you are to show it by the good conversation (way you live) in meekness. The more wisdom and knowledge you have been given, the more meekness you must walk in. God does not give you His wisdom and knowledge to live the way you desire, but to practice daily what you say, and walk in humility while you are living it.

Walking in meekness have a way of allowing others to receive what you say, because you are not walking in your pride. The more wisdom God gives you, the more you should ask God to keep you humble and obedient, to continue in His will.

1) - When others can see that you are anointed by God to walk in His wisdom, and see you humbly obey whatever God instructs you

to do, they will follow your leadership in Christ (Philippians 3:17 - Brethren, be followers together of me, and mark them which walk so as ye have us for an example). Paul was able to instruct others to follow him, and the others, who were walking the gospel and not just talking it. He was very anointed by God, but he was just as humble as he was anointed. Paul was mature enough to know that everything he had attained (achieved) and obtained (to succeed in gaining possessions) came directly from God. The power that rested inside of him, was God's power. Therefore, he had no right to boast or walk proudly and arrogantly. Because of this, humility and obedience became his daily spiritual garments, and he wore them well.

2) - You cannot walk in obedience and meekness if your mind has not been changed to the mind of Christ, it does no matter how hard you try (Philippians 2:5 - Let this mind be in you, which was also in Christ Jesus). Having the mind of Christ, will surely be the force behind your spiritual meekness and your obedience to Him. Jesus had the mind to do His Father's will at all times. With the mind of Christ, you will have the same desire to do the will of God. This kind of meekness and obedience is pure and divine because it is given through the Holy Spirit. You cannot earn it on your own. You must allow the Holy Spirit to work in you, the will of God. Humbly obey God and watch your spiritual meekness mature.

3) - A Christian's life and speech should display the fact that you have been walking with Jesus (Acts 4:13 - Now when they saw the boldness of Peter and John, and perceived that they were unlearned and ignorant men, they marvelled; and they took knowledge of them, that they had been with Jesus). Someone besides you, should be able to know that you are truly an obedient, meek, and loving Christian, by the way you carry yourself. There should be no doubt about some things regarding you and your lifestyle. Your life should be so fine tuned in Christ, that you will be like a symphony playing on one accord, by the way you are living, speaking, and spiritually working in your call. You should be playing the same tune, over and over again. Let your light shine and show others how to walk in obedience and meekness as you serve Jesus Christ.

***This week, allow the Holy Spirit to help you address things in your life, that may be hindering your spiritual fruit of meekness from maturing. Then obey Him and perform what is necessary to mature.

Remember, obedience and meekness is needed, to walk humbly in the wisdom of God.

Days 26 - 30

Why is Meekness so Important?

Scripture Text

Galatians 5:22a-23

[22a)-]But the fruit of the Spirit is: [23)-]Meekness, temperance: against such there is no law.

In this last week of maturing the spiritual fruit of meekness, I would like to take a moment to explain why **Meekness** is so important. As a fruit of the Spirit, it is the true source of caring for others in a heartfelt way. This is God's requirement for all Christians. It should also be included as part of your daily way of living. There is a certain way the Lord wants His Church to present herself to the world.

Meekness is so important, because it is included in God's Holy Spirit, to be used by the believers in time of need. The Christians, in the spirit of gentleness, kindness, humility, self-control, tenderness, and consideration, would be able to help others, as they face life issues. **Please note, this is a fruit that comes totally from the Holy Spirit, so everybody does not have it.** In many situations, through the cares of life, this fruit will help each individual to be kind and gentle people. Meekness is needed in every walk of life, to help someone or for someone to help you.

This last year has been especially hard on all of us, and many people has suffered so many things. There have been so many loses of so many people and things. People are broken, crushed, and so very discouraged. Some need help in every area of their life. The spirit of meekness is in high demand from one to another.

The operation of the Spirit of Meekness is needed now more than ever before. Can you see why so many people need the Spirit of Meekness?

1) - Compassion - Deep awareness of the sufferings of others coupled with the wish to relieve it. (People need help and relief from their sufferings. We offer them Jesus and we also give them compassion).

2) - Gentleness - Considerate and kind; Not harsh or severe; mild and soft. (In times like these we need Jesus, we also need a friend to show us kindness).

3) - Humble - Marked by meekness or modesty in behavior, attitude, or spirit; not arrogant or prideful. (It is time to humble ourselves and minister to the needs of others. Jesus called Christians to be servants to all people).

4) - Tenderness - Marked by or expressing gentle emotions, loving. (Now is not the time to be so hard on everyone. Show the tender mercies of God, to all people and help the healing process begin).

5) - Self-Control - Control of one's emotions, desires, or actions by one's own will. (Sure, is easy to display uncontrolled behavior in every area of your life right now, because of the pain you are suffering. But take the time to show and direct others to the hope that you have in Christ Jesus. They really need this from you).

6) - Sympathy - The act or power of sharing the feelings of another; A feeling or an expression of pity or sorrow for the distress of another. (Please, do not act as though you do not see the pain and sufferings of others. Show your sympathy for others as they attempt to deal with their pain and sufferings. Also pray for them and help them if you are able to do so).

7) - Empathy - Identification with and understanding of another's situation, feelings, and motives. (Do not sit in judgment of others, because you do not know the whole story behind the situation. Pray for them and allow God to do what His will is for the individual. Remember your part is to identify with them and show understanding for their situation. God's job is to fix it).

In today's society it is hard to find many people who can be gentle and kind to others. There is such a shortage in patience, love, compassion, sympathy, and empathy for others. The Christians have been filled with the Holy Spirit of God to make these virtues active in the world and the Church. Even when the world cannot show this kindness and gentleness, the Christians are to be living this way.

Meekness is so important to keep the love of God flowing from heart to heart in this world. If the world were to go on without the Spirit of Meekness present, what kind of world and people would we all become. Think about what it would be like to walk the streets without kindness operating on some level? Who would be left to care for God's people?

*** This week think on these things, and decide if you are ready to mature your fruit of meekness. Allow God to mature your spiritual fruit of meekness now.

Remember, it is time to walk in the Spirit of God, to help bring the healing that is so needed in this world. Can God depend on your for your service in the Spirit of Meekness?

NOTES

Month Twelve - Maturing the Fruit of Temperance

Days 1 - 5

What is Temperance?

Scripture Text

1Corinthians 9:24-27

**24)-Know ye not that they which run in a race run all, but one
receiveth the prize? So run, that ye may obtain. 25)-And every man
that striveth for the mastery is temperate in all things. Now they
do it to obtain a corruptible crown; but we an incorruptible. 26)-I
therefore so run, not as uncertainly; so, fight I, not as one that
beateth the air: 27)-But I keep under my body, and bring it into
subjection: lest that by any means, when I have preached to others,
I myself should be a castaway.**

What is Temperance? Temperance is moderation and self restraint, as in behavior. It is the ability to master and control the body (flesh) with all of its lust. Such lusts as desires, passion, appetite, sensual urges, and cravings.

In this Scripture the Apostle Paul is using the language of a race, to describe the type of actions needed to participate to win the contest, and not to just run in the race. He knew that in a race all could enter and run, but only one would win the prize. He wanted to be the one to win. So, he never started an assignment for Christ, without the attitude to win by completion of the task. Knowing that the only way to please his God, would be to complete the assignments.

Now he is encouraging the Christians, to enter into their relationship with Jesus Christ to win, nothing else will do. Starting their walk with the Lord, means nothing if they do not stay the course and finish strong.

He is saying that every man who striveth (exert much effort or energy; endeavor; contend; fight forcefully), must be temperate (exercising moderation and self- restraint) so that he may win. The natural man when he is competing, he competes for the natural prize. Christians compete for a prize that is not corruptible but eternal. Sure, you will receive natural benefits also, but the grand prize is eternal life.

1) - This should raise the bar of temperance to a higher level, for all who are in it to win. You are not running this race as if you do not know the prize, but because you know what the grand prize is, you give it all you have at all times ([26)]-I therefore so run, not as uncertainly; so, fight I, not as one that beateth the air:). You are not serving God just to be doing it, but to receive the gift of eternal life, and to live the abundant life that goes with the prize. This calls for having self-control, up and operating fully in your entire life. Get busy maturing this fruit.

2) - Paul was very careful as to how he walked or lived for God. He knew that it was possible for him to convince others to run well and if he did not have self-control, he could very well lose his rewards ([27)]-But I keep under my body and bring it into subjection: lest that by any means, when I have preached to others, I myself should be a castaway). This Scripture teaches you, that if you do not have control of your fleshly behaviors, you can tell everyone else how to live, and you may be the one to miss the mark. Please do not tell people how to live if you are not able to control your own cravings. If you cannot control it, what testimonies will you have to convince others that they should have the power to do so? Show them by your walk, not just your talk. You must show the power of God's Spirit.

3) - Temperance is a very important fruit of the Spirit. Is teaches and gives you the ability to bring your body into subjection to the will of God (Romans 6:12 - Let not sin therefore reign in your mortal body, that ye should obey it in the lusts thereof). When you have temperance, you are strong, controlled, and restrained to the cravings of your flesh. Do not yield unto temptations, instead resist it and you will be victorious as you walk with Christ. It is when you yield, you fall into trouble getting weaker and weaker. When you resist, you become stronger and stronger as you please God. Desire to be strong in the Lord and in the power of His might! The more you resist, the stronger you become in that area. **Temperance is control in action.**

***This is the first week of temperance. Take the time to locate your areas of weakness and begin to resist the urges and cravings whenever they arise.

Remember, you have the power of the Holy Spirit inside of you, to help you resist every temptation that arises in your life. Start now resisting the pull!

Days 6 - 10

I Must Be in Control of My Body

Scripture Text

1 Corinthians 6:19-20

19)-What? Know ye not that your body is the temple of the Holy Ghost, which is in you, which ye have of God, and ye are not your own? 20)-For ye are bought with a price: therefore, glorify God in your body, and in your spirit, which are God's.

One of the many struggles that Christians have in their walk with Christ, is the ability to control their very own bodies. The problem is not that it cannot be done, but you must do certain things as required in the Scriptures, to make it happen. When you walk in a constant awareness that God Spirit lives inside of you, that He is Holy as God the Father is Holy, you will start to reject the unholy things in your walk (body). Always keep your mind in remembrance of the fact that God is the owner of your body and your spirit. You do not own yourself, you were bought with a price by the Almighty God through the blood shedding of His Son, Jesus Christ. So, your body does not belong to you, but to the Lord God Almighty.

To keep you body pure and holy, start connecting the dots to the fact that your body is the temple or Church of the Living God. Yes, you may go to a building to worship, but your true temple is the body that houses the Spirit of God. Also, that God is living in your body and using you to complete His work in this earth. This alone should convince you of the need to control your lustful desires. As you are conscious of the ever abiding (presence) of the Holy Spirit living inside of you and how much He hates sin, you will resist sin. This will show how much you really love, honor, trust, obey, and respect your Father who is in Heaven. This is how you glorify God in your body and your spirit.

1) - It is not about how many Scriptures you may know, but about how many Scriptures you are living. We are instructed by the word of God to be a doer of the word and not a hearer only (James 1:22-24 - [22)]-But be ye doers of the word, and not hearers only, deceiving your own selves. [23)]-For if any be a hearer of the word, and not a doer, he is like unto a man beholding his natural face in a glass:[24)]-For he beholdeth himself, and goeth his way, and straightway forgetteth what manner of man he was). James was one of Jesus' natural brothers. He knew more about Jesus than any of the other Apostles who walked with Him, because He lived with Jesus. He saw and knew the life of His brother. Therefore, He knew that walking in Jesus, meant that you were a producer of works and fruit. No, works do not save you, but it does show who you really are in Christ Jesus. James understood very well, that your life, the way you obeyed, and your ability to bear fruit, was the evidence of your walk with the Lord. After hearing the word of God, the evidence will show up in the way your life has changed, and the way you continue on in the Faith. When you are doing the word of God, you will not forget what manner of man you are, because you are sure of your new spirit in Christ Jesus. Every Christian must show and walk in self-control to be effective in your witness. When you walk in the flesh, others will also know it.

2) - To glorify God, is to pull off your old man of sin, and walk in the newness of life in Christ Jesus. You have been born again and cannot live in sin any longer (Romans 6:1-2 - [1)]-What shall we say then? Shall we continue in sin, that grace may abound? [2)]-God forbid. How shall we, that are dead to sin, live any longer therein?). Believers are dead to sin. Meaning they are not practicing sinners anymore. Sure, you may fall short from time to time, but that does know mean you should continue walking in sin. The apostle Paul asked the question "How shall we, that are dead to sin, live any longer therein?" **He wanted the believers to understand that if you have been born again, you are a new creature, old things are passed away, and all things are new (1 Corinthians 5:17 - Therefore if any man be in Christ, he is a new creature: old**

things are passed away, behold, all things are become new). This is so powerful to know because you have been given a fresh start, and the hold that sin once had on you, has been cut off, you are no longer in bondage to sin. With the Holy Spirit living inside of you, empowering your walk to live the new life God has given unto you. Walk in the newness of life in the spiritual fruit of temperance **"Self-Control."**

3) - God wants you to glorify Him in your body and in your spirit (1Corinthians 6:20b - [20b)-]Therefore glorify God in your body, and in your spirit, which are God's). Christians must always know that God wants more than your spirit. He wants your body and your mind. In fact, God wants all of you, that is why He said your body is not your own for you are bought with a price. How can you belong to God, and allow yourself to be shared with God's enemy, the devil? You are not to give portions of you to Satan and the other part to God. God wants all of you, after all, this is what He paid for with the blood of His Son. Give all of you to God. Do not allow the enemy to touch your body. **Self-Control teaches you to walk away from the sins of your flesh as listed in (Galatians 5:19-21a - [19)-]Now the works of the flesh are manifest, which are these: Adultery, fornication, uncleanness, lasciviousness, [20)-]Idolatry, witchcraft, hatred, variance, emulations, wrath, strife, seditions, heresies, [21a)-]Envyings, murders, drunkenness, revellings, and such like).** To walk with Christ, you must be in control of your body, because you cannot teach or tell anyone else to be in control of their bodies, when they see and know that you are out of control. Please bring your body into subjection to the will of God, allow the Holy Spirit to help you mature your spiritual fruit of self-control. To be out of control will always make you shame of your walk with Christ. Take the time to resist the temptations of the flesh and walk in the Spirit of God daily. Start resisting the cravings and desires of you flesh. Desire to grow in your walk with Christ. Mature that fruit!

***This is one of those weeks, when you know that you must rise up and live the life you were meant to live in God. You cannot continue to deceive yourself regarding these issues. Your body belong to God everyday!

Remember, only you, with the help of the Holy Spirit, can make this spiritual fruit of self-control a part of who you really are. Just Do It!

Days 11 - 15

I Must Grow in Self-Control

Scripture Text

2Peter 1:6,8

6)-And to knowledge temperance; and to temperance patience; and to patience godliness; 8)-For if these things be in you, and abound, they make you that ye shall neither be barren nor unfruitful in the knowledge of our Lord Jesus Christ.

While learning about the spiritual fruit, it is amazing to see how they all work together. As you mature in one, you must not stop there but continue to grow in the others because they are not separate, it is one fruit (the fruit of the Spirit is). Please note this is one fruit, so it must have maturity in all areas.

This reminds me of how the natural body operates. As you begin to grow up, all parts of you must also grow to keep a balance, in the way every part of you mature and operate. Each part of your body has certain responsibilities that it is to carry out on a daily basis. If each part does not mature as it should, you can have malfunctions that may cause many problems in your life, later on. Maturing of your body, mind, and spirit is a necessary process of life. So is maturing your spiritual fruit, a necessary part of your spiritual life.

If you pay close attention to the progression of your body maturing, sometimes you can fix the part that is having issues. But if you let it go too long, there may not be much help to give. The same can be true of your spiritual fruit in the maturing process. If you allow the Holy Spirit access to do whatever needs to be done at the time needed, you will experience maturity at the right time, in the spiritual fruit. You cannot make your fruit mature on your own, you will need the Holy Spirit to do it by producing the right situations to mature them. I keep stressing the fact that you cannot do it on your own, so you will know to depend on, and allow the Holy Spirit to help and lead you to spiritual maturity.

Temperance is also a fruit that will need your cooperation to mature. If you do not agree with the Holy Spirit when He is working in this area of your life, to mature self-control, you will keep yielding to temptations. Making excuses because you keep failing in that same situation, will then become a crutch for you. You must add knowledge to temperance, to temperance, add patience, and to patience, add godliness. There is a reason for this information to be given in Scripture. Maturing must not happen in only one area, it needs to happen even in the most difficult areas of your life. When you live and walk in knowledge, self-control, patience, and godliness to your character, will give you a life of fruitfulness in the knowledge of Jesus Christ our Lord. This should be what you are living for.

1) - When you are living daily with temperance in action, others will see your good work and glorify God (Matthew 5:14; 16 - [14)]-Ye are the light of the world. A city that is set on a hill cannot be hid. [16)]-Let your light so shine before men, that they may see your good works, and glorify your father which is in heaven). Your life will become more rewarding to you and others, because you are pleasing God in your body. Walking in self-control is something that others are sure to take notice of. When you are out of control, it affects your behavior in most cases, causing others to doubt your relationship with God. The Lord wants others to see your good works and give glory to Him, for what he can do in the lives of His people. Without self-control you can have a lot of bad issues with people and a bad reputation that may cause others to reject your witness about Jesus. Please do not allow your lack of temperance to damage your witness for the Lord.

2) -You must be in control of your tongue at all times. The tongue can cause so much trouble in your life, and if not controlled, you can

live to regret much of its actions (James 3:5-6 - 5)-Even so the tongue is a little member, and boasteth great things. Behold, how great a matter a little fire kindleth. 6)-And the tongue is a fire, a world of iniquity: so is the tongue amongst our members, that it defileth the whole body, and setteth on fire the course of nature; and it is set on fire of hell). This Scripture teaches the severity of a tongue that is out of control. It is one of the smaller members of the body, but it carries a lot of weight. If your tongue is out of control, it can cause you so many heartaches and pain. It can break up so many relationships, and cause much harm to others. Self-control is needed constantly in speech, and integrity of your tongue. This tongue that I am speaking about, should not be the tongue of the Christians. Your tongue, if not controlled, can cause more damage in people's life than you may ever be able to fix. With this in mind, please get control of your tongue. **Your tongue should be able to keep you out of trouble and not in trouble (Proverbs 21:23 - Who so keepeth his mouth and his tongue; keepeth his soul from troubles).** This cannot be stated any plainer, self-control, keeps your soul. Out of control, destroys your soul. Consider, do you have control of your tongue or does your tongue have control of you? You are not the only one who can answer this question. Others will know whether or not you can control your tongue by the way you talk. I often say, "if you want to really know someone, be quiet long enough to listen to them." Their speech will tell you all you need to know, **Control or Out of Control!**

3) - Self-control will define the way you live as a Christian. You can say all you desire to say but people actually watch your life (Proverbs 16:32 - He that is slow to anger is better than the mighty; And he that ruleth his spirit than he that taketh a city). What is your life saying about you, to others and to your God? Proverbs say if you are able to control your anger you are better than the mighty. Why? Because there are many great people who have done great things, but are not able to control their anger, therefore it destroys relationships on many levels. Also, if you can control your spirit and stay within the boundaries of God's will, you are greater than the person who takes over a city, because you allow God to rule your life. If you have not been resisting temptations, now is the time to start, and your fruit will grow.

***Use this week to grow in self-control in all areas of your life. Do not just think about it but make a conscious decision to do it.

Remember, you have the power of the Almighty God living on the inside of you and He can help you do it!

Days 16 - 20

I Will Control My Cravings and Desires

Scripture Text

1 John 2:15-16

15)-Love not the world, neither the things that are in the world. If any man love the world, the love of the Father is not in him. 16)-For all that is in the world, the lust of the flesh, and the lust of the eyes, and the pride of life, is not of the Father, but is of the world.

In these Scriptures we are instructed to love not the world, neither the things that are in the world. This does not mean that you are to hate the world or the things that God created in the world. You are not to love the world system (the way it operates) and the sinful behaviors and lusts of this world. You are not to love and desire, the cravings and doings that are the production of sin, that is happening in this world. Yes, you are to take care of and thank God for His creation, but to desire the lusts and cravings that are the rebelling against God, is what you must not love. You must resist all of its' sinfulness.

You are to understand that if you fall in love with the lusts, cravings, and desires of the world, it will draw you away from God and His will for your life. We are more than the body, we are mind and spirit also. To invest in body only is cheating your mind and spirit. If you fall in love with the things that are of the world, all it does is create a desire for more and more. You will never get enough, there will always be a craving and a desire for more, and the cravings pushes you to want more, and more. There is no end to the cravings of the world system.

You must be filled with the Spirit of God to combat these lusts, cravings, and desires. You must be born again, not just professing Christ, but actually living for the Lord (Philippians 1:11 - Being

filled with the fruits of righteousness, which are by Jesus Christ unto the glory and praise of God). If you do not have the active spiritual fruit of temperance (self-Control) in your life, you will begin to do and desire these things. If you love all these things of the world, the love of the Father is not in you. It is hard to serve God and the strong cravings, desires, and lusts of the world system. God must have your loyalty first, and these things will not be so important and time consuming in your life. That is why, God is to be first. Is God truly first in your life and can you resist the cravings of the world?

All that is in the world is:

1) - The lusts of the flesh - Involves, touching, smelling, tasting, hearing, seeing, and feeling. These are your desires, urges, and cravings. They are not wrong in themselves because we need them for a normal life. But it is the lack of self-control that makes it sinful. When you are lusting, craving, and desiring things that are forbidden by God, that makes it sinful. Being filled with the Holy Spirit will teach and help you control the urges and place standards and boundaries in your life. Also, the Holy Spirit will help you to avoid overindulgence (unrestrained gratification, always wanting more and more) and license (lack of due restraint, heedlessness for the precepts of proper behavior). This is not just fornication and adultery, but all of the sinful acts of the flesh as mentioned in **Galatians 5:19-21 (Please take the time to read all of these works of the flesh this week).**

The Holy Spirit has the power to keep you walking in the spirit, so that you will not give in to and allow your flesh to overrule your spirit, and walk with Christ (Galatians 5:16-18 - 16)-This I say then, walk in the Spirit, and ye shall not fulfill the lust of the flesh. 17)-For the flesh lusteth against the Spirit, and the Spirit against the flesh: and these are contrary the one to the other: so, you cannot do the things that ye would. 18)-But if ye be led of the Spirit, ye are not under the law). You must have the Holy Spirit inside of you leading, guiding, and helping you to mature your fruit of self-control.

2) - The lusts of the eyes - You use your eyes to see and there is nothing wrong with that. God gave you eyes to see, and this is normal. It is also normal to want what you see at times. The problem starts when you want what is forbidden by God. There are so many things that falls into this category, and it constantly trap you into wanting what you cannot and should not have.

Do you remember before you became a Christian, whenever you gave in to temptations, you would possibly say "Lord if you just get me out of this, I will not do it again"? However, no sooner than you get out of the situation you find yourself doing the same thing again and again. You tried but you did not possess the power of spiritual self-control in your life to stay faithful and quit. The Holy Spirit is given to help you stay steadfast and unmovable in self-control. You may be able to quit for a while, one day unexpectedly you find yourself back in the same situation. This should help you to understand that without the Holy Spirit in your life, you are not able to make yourself quit sinning.

Now that you are a Christian, you must not allow this lust of the eyes to pull you out of your lane in Christ. You must allow the Holy Spirit to keep your eyes from the lusts of the eyes (2 Peter 2:14 - Having eyes full of adultery and that cannot cease from sin; beguiling (to deceive or cheat) unstable souls: a heart they have exercised with covetous practices; cursed children).

Just to name a few:

1) - The lust of the eyes for sex and different types of pleasures

2) - Wanting someone else's spouse

3) - Looking at a woman or man with wrong sexual desires

4) - Looking at what someone possess and wanting it for yourself

5) - Many other desires of the eyes to be looked upon for sinful pleasures

You must protect your eyes through the power of the Holy Spirit of God, daily!

3) - The pride of life - This is selfishness at all levels. This is the person who is totally consumed with himself/herself. Everything is all about you, and what you want, it is almost never about someone else (Romans 12:16 - Be of the same mind one towards another. Mind not high things but condescend (come to the level of people whom you feel is inferior to you) to men of low estate. Be not wise in your own conceits (high opinion of your own ability and worth). Do not be that person who always needs attention, give space for others to shine. People who are selfish will seek attention in many areas of their lives such as:

1) - want others to honor them

2) - seek to have power over others

3) - wants recognition for everything they do

4) - always looks for others to compliment how they look and dress

5) - always wants the best positions and the best of everything

6) - the individual tries to outshine everybody, etc.

Also, the pride of life deals with arrogance, self-sufficient, and boasting all about oneself. Remember, this person thinks that everything is about him/her. There is not room for many others in their life. You can be able to control the members of your body, and allow yourself to please the Almighty God as you walk with Him in grace. Know that temperance can be a reality in your life, and you will walk in the joy of the Lord as this fruit matures.

***Please take this week to allow the Holy Spirit, to aide you in the maturity of your self-control fruit. When you look at the picture painted in this week's teachings, ask yourself "do I want to be like this?"

This is very important and must be taken very seriously. Yield not to temptations, avoid it at all costs.

Remember, just listen, and obey the voice of the Holy Spirit, to stay in control of who God created you to be. Never lose control of who you really are in Christ.

Days 21 - 25

I Have Power Over My Body

Scripture Text

Romans 12:1-2

1)-I beseech you brethren, by the mercies of God, that ye present your bodies a living sacrifice, holy, acceptable unto God, which is your reasonable service. 2)-And be not conformed to this world: but be ye transformed by the renewing of your mind, that ye may prove what is that good, and acceptable, and perfect will of God.

This is strong teaching regarding your body. This Scripture is urging or begging the believer to present or give your body to God as a living sacrifice. Meaning to give God complete and total rule and authority, in and over your body. When you give God this type of permission and authority to your body and life, this will guarantee self-control of your body. I am persuaded that no one else can control or teach you how to control your body and life, like the Almighty God who Created you. God knows more about you than you will ever know about yourself.

You are His signature work, because of this, He knows what to do and how to bring your body into subjection to His will. God would never ask you to give your body to Him on this level if it were not possible to do. It is because of His divine love for you, that He urges you to give Him control of your body. God loves your body more than you do because He is the maker of your body.

1) - God wants your body to be Holy, meaning, set apart unto Him and Him alone. When you give God your body, being reserved only for Him, He will do great and mighty things in your life (1 Peter 1:16 - Because it is written, be ye holy: for I am holy). Because God is Holy, set apart and above everything He created, He is now asking you to be set apart unto Him. He wants to complete the purpose in your life that you were created to perform. God knows that you will never be able to fulfill this tall order on your own, so He is urging you to give your body to Him, and let Him do this great thing in your life for you. What loving and caring God you serve. There is none like unto Him in all the earth.

2) - The presentation of your body being Holy unto God, must also be acceptable unto Him, and it cannot be done the way you want to do it. You must follow the directions of God to be acceptable unto Him (Matthew 16:24 - Then said Jesus unto His disciples, if any man will come after me, let him deny himself, and take up his cross, and follow me). Jesus knew that you would not be able to follow Him, if you could not deny yourself. Selfishness is not to be a part of the Christian's relationship with God. This is one of the first step to gaining self-control over your body and life. When you can walk in the will of God, fulfilling God's will for your life, you cannot be selfish. You are sent into the world to make disciples for Him, and it will require you leaving your will to complete His will. Self-control is much needed in this area, because you will be asked to drop you and your will to complete God's will. Having your body set apart unto God will allow you to do the will of God. You belong to Him. **You must walk by faith to please Him, putting all your trust in God and waiting for Him to direct your course (Hebrews 11:6a - But without faith it is impossible to please Him).** Being selfish and out of control, will not let the will of God happen in your life.

God is not asking you for no more than your reasonable service. After all Jesus did for you, can you not give Him your service of being set apart to Him and to Him alone. Why should God have to share you with other gods? Give yourself to God.

3) - The only way to start or continue being an acceptable, holy, living sacrifice unto God, is to have a transformed mind. You cannot have the mind to pursue after the world system and belong to God (Romans 12:2 - And be not conformed to this world: but be ye transformed by the renewing of your mind, that ye may prove what

is that good, and acceptable, and perfect will of God). When you are a Christian, it is so important that your mind agrees with the changes that have been implemented in your heart by the Holy Spirit. Now that you have a new Spirit, you must begin the process of transforming your way of thinking and the way you see and respond to life. This will not happen all at once or over night, but the process should start immediately. Start reading the word of God (Bible) daily to learn of the things of God. You cannot change your mind if you do not know what needs to change. The Scriptures will teach you about all the things required of you by God. You will learn about love, peace, joy, forgiveness, longsuffering, faithfulness, self-control, and many other things, that were not so important in your old way of living. You may not have given much thought as to why this is so important, but I would like to point out one major reason to transform your mind and have the mind of Christ now.

You are empowered with the nine fruits of the Spirit to teach and help you to live a holy life. If you do not transform you mind to agree with the Holy Spirit, you will find yourself overriding everything the Holy Spirit tells you to do. This will cause serious problems with the maturing of your spiritual fruit, that is needed to help you walk, talk, and live as a genuine Christian. Self-control is a fruit you must not allow to be immature. If this fruit does not mature, you will find yourself walking and living contrary to the will of God. Your love for God should prompt you to desire to have Self-control operating at its fullest potential, because you want to please God with all that is within you.

***This week study the word of God with all your heart. Pray from the sincerity of your heart, and trust God to help and teach you to mature your spiritual fruit of Temperance (self-control). Your life really does depend on this.

Remember, God gave you your body. You are to honor and glorify God with your body and your spirit!

Days 26 - 30

The Spiritual Fruit of Temperance (Self-Control)

Scripture Text

Galatians 5:22-23

22)-But the fruit of the Spirit is love, joy, peace, longsuffering, gentleness, goodness, faith, 23)-Meekness, temperance: against such there is no law.

This is the last week of teachings on the fruit of the Spirit. We are ending with the fruit of Temperance. Sometimes when things are listed last, people have the tendency to think that it is not as important as the previous ones. This is not true concerning temperance. This fruit is just as important as the other eight because it is given at the same time, by the same Spirit, and for the same purpose. To empower you to be the Christian God always intended you to be.

Each fruit was given to handle certain areas of your life, and temperance was given for the same purpose. Temperance is needed to restrain the Christian from sinful desires, lusts, cravings, and behaviors. Also, it is needed to teach and help you to honor God with your body, soul, and spirit, in every walk of your life.

Each Christian is responsible for growing and maturing the fruit of the Spirit in his/her life. This is achieved by obeying, yielding, honoring, and hearing the Holy Spirit. Having self-control operating in your life, will give you the perseverance you need to stay the course and complete your divine assignments given by God. You will not complete assignments if you do not walk in self-control.

Because you cannot rule the Holy Spirit, you must depend on Him to direct your entire course of living. Self-control is needed to keep you walking and dedicated in your relationship with God. Without this great fruit you will be totally out of control. The more your fruit matures the more self-control you will operate in.

1) - The spiritual fruit of self-control is needed in Christian conduct. It does not matter what office you may hold, you are still required to walk in temperance (Titus2:11-13 - 11)-For the grace of God that bringeth salvation hath appeared to all men, 12)-Teaching us that denying ungodliness and worldly lusts we should live soberly, righteously, and godly, in this present world: 13)-Looking for that blessed hope, and the glorious appearing of the great God and our Savior Jesus Christ). Christians are to be instructed and trained, to deny ungodliness and worldly lusts, and live soberly, righteous and godly in this present world. This will not be accomplished in you without the power and authority of the Holy Spirit. The Scriptures will teach and train you how to walk away from worldly lusts and ungodliness. Through the instructions and trainings, you must rely on the power of God to work through you for deliverance. Self-control is the only way to walk this out in real time. This makes you dependent on the Spirit of God everyday of your life. God wants you to lean and depend totally on Him.

The reason to allow God to work His will in your life, is because of the blessed hope of His return. You are to make disciples for Christ. How can you make disciples if you are not a dedicated, self-controlled, disciple yourself? You really need to operate daily in this fruit. It will give you the confidence you need in Christ.

2) - Self-control is needed to stay in the race for eternal life. If you cannot continue this race in temperance, you may be disqualified (1 Corinthians 9:25-27 - 25)-And every man that striveth for the mastery is temperate in all things. Now they do it to obtain a corruptible crown, but we an incorruptible. 26)-I therefore so run, not as uncertainly: so, fight I, not as one that beateth in the air: 27)-But I keep under my body, and bring it into subjection: lest that by any means, when I have preached to others, I myself should be a

castaway). The apostle Paul knew the power of self-control, and he lived in it. He knew what it took to stay committed to his God and the call on his life. Paul compared the Christian's life to that of an accomplished athlete who was working for the mastery (top level) by being temperate in all things (total self-control in every area of life). They do it in the natural body to obtain their greatest heart's desire, to be the top winner. They sacrificed everything to gain that one thing. Paul was encouraging the Christians to do the same thing for their walk with Christ. You are to bring your body into subjection, keep it under self-control, so that you will not be disqualified in the race of life. He said that he did this, knowing that when he had preached to others to do what was right, and he failed to have self-control in his own life, he could be a castaway.

You must understand that sin will always be here, but you do not have to serve sin. You must fight the battle against sin so you will not lose your reward. Please humble yourself to the direction of the Holy Spirit and refuse to yield to the demands of your flesh.

3) - The fruit of the Spirit is the very nature of God. Every Believer is to walk and live every day to grow closer and closer to Him. The closer you walk with God the more you become like Him (Ephesians 5:15-20 - 15)-See then that ye walk circumspectly, not as fools, but as wise, 16)-Redeeming the time, because the days are evil. 17)-Wherefore be ye not unwise but understanding what the will of the Lord is. 18)-And be not drunk with wine, wherein is excess; but be filled with the Spirit; 19)-Speaking to yourselves in psalms and hymns and spiritual songs, singing and making melody in your heart to the Lord; 20)-Giving thanks always for all things unto God and the Father in the name of our Lord Jesus Christ). These Scriptures teaches you how to walk closely with God. You are to walk circumspectly (heedful of circumstances) not as someone acting foolish but taking heed as a wise person. Keeping in touch with reality, knowing that evil is increasing day by day. Do not be unwise but understand what the will of God is for your life. Do not live in excess or out of control but be filled with the Spirit.

When you are filled with the Spirit, you are also filled with the fruit of the Spirit. The Spirit and His fruit are inseparable, they come together. Being filled with this powerful pair, keep on feeding the Spirit with psalms, hymns, spiritual songs, and singing, making melody in your heart, where the Holy Spirit lives inside of you. These instructions will keep you in perfect peace and walking in total self-control, producing in you a spirit of thanksgiving unto God the Father, God the Son, and God the Holy Spirit.

***The conclusion to the whole matter is to love God with all your heart, soul, and might. You are to walk daily in the mature fruit of the Spirit, to bring glory to your Lord and Savior Jesus Christ. The powerful fruit of the Spirit will help you mature as a healthy Christian, able to produce fruit for the kingdom of God. As you learn to walk in the Spirit of God and allow the fruit of the Spirit to mature in you, you will be enabled to bear fruit as required in John 15:1-6 (our starting Scriptures).

As you stay connected to the true vine, Jesus Christ, your spiritual fruit will mature, and you will be very productive in bearing fruit for your God. The Spiritual fruit and the bearing of fruit are tied together. If you are not walking and abiding in the Holy Spirit, allowing the fruit of the spirit to mature, how can you produce fruit for God's Kingdom? **(Galatians 5:22-23 - [22)]-But the fruit of the Spirit is love, joy, peace, longsuffering, gentleness, goodness, faith, [23)]-Meekness, temperance: against such there is no law).**

***You the Christian, need the Spirit of Christ to abide in you, so that you can walk in the Spirit and not in the flesh. You will then become productive in fruit bearing!

Remember, John 15:3-4 [3)]-Now ye are clean through the word which I have spoken unto you. [4)]-Abide in me, and I in you. As the branch (Christian) cannot bear fruit of itself, except it abide in the vine (Jesus), no more can ye, except ye abide in me.

***Spiritual fruit maturing means great production seasons in your fruit bearing processes, as you journey through your walk with Jesus Christ as a Christian!**

NOTES

CPSIA information can be obtained
at www.ICGtesting.com
Printed in the USA
LVHW090722210122
708888LV00001B/13

9 781638 718574